sew teen

Make Your Own Cool Clothes

Sheila Zent

sixth&spring books

Sixth&Spring Books
233 Spring Street
New York, New York 10013

Editorial Director
Trisha Malcolm

Art Director
Chi Ling Moy

Graphic Designers
Nancy Sabato
Sheena Paul

Stylist
Laura Maffeo

Associate Editor
Erin Walsh

Instructions Editor
Susan Huxley

Photography
Dan Howell

Book Division Manager
Erica Smith

Production Manager
David Joinnides

President and Publisher, Sixth&Spring Books
Art Joinnides

Library of Congress Control Number: 2005934948
ISBN: 1-931543-90-9
ISBN-13: 978-1-931543-90-3

1   3   5   7   9   10   8   6   4   2
Manufactured in China

dedication

This book is dedicated to all teens and almost-teens who suffer from boredom. If you spend your free time watching the tube, surfing the net and yakking on the phone but still need something fun to do, get ready to turn the page.

Sewing is where your ideas come alive. It provides a canvas for your creative urges. Completing a project makes you feel good about yourself. When you wear your new creation, it makes your parents proud (and your friends a little jealous). Sewing can help you figure out who you are. But mostly, sewing is fun. This is for you.

table of contents

Anyone can become a fashion designer by combining a creative idea with some basic sewing skills. Build your resumé as you complete each new project.

introduction

if you picked up this book, chances are good that something about sewing caught your eye. Whether you already sew or would like to learn, sewing is a fun way to spend your free time. It's *the ultimate creative activity*.

Imagine taking several pieces of fabric that are cut into different shapes and sizes. One by one you piece them together until, almost magically, they become a top or purse or skirt—practically in front of your eyes. What started as an idea is now something real that you can show off by wearing it, using it, or giving it as a gift.

Sewing gives you complete control over fabrics, colors and textures, as well as the fit and appearance of the finished item. While you fine-tune your personal style, you can create clothes and accessories that express your feelings and ideas. Plus, no one will ever be wearing the same thing as you.

If you're just starting out, take it slow. Don't be surprised if you find a little math here or there, but it's not hard. Honest. Don't get discouraged if something you're working on gets confusing or doesn't turn out quite the way that you wanted it to.

Every top fashion designer started somewhere and made plenty of mistakes along the way to success. Stay true to your ideas, and your skills will catch up. Above all, have fun and be proud of your original creation.

Whether sewing is one of your favorite hobbies, or you are just starting to stitch, look over this section that explains all the basic tools, terms and techniques you'll need to complete your project with great results.

tools

To make the projects in this book, you'll need most of the tools on the list that follows.

If you're starting out, don't spend a fortune on fancy (or expensive) stuff. You don't need a top-of-the-line sewing machine or super-good dressmaker scissors. As you get more into sewing, upgrade your equipment and tools a little at a time.

- Big safety pin for threading elastic or drawstring through a casing.

- Calculator with a percentage button.

- Dressmaker pencil that makes marks that disappear, either water-soluble (marks wash away when dabbed with a damp cloth) or air-soluble (marks fade automatically after a few days).

- Hand-sewing needles in a variety of sizes.

- Iron that has a steam setting.

- Pen closed with a retracted point or a pencil with a broken point for pushing out fabric corners when you turn them inside out.

- Pencil, the ordinary variety.

- Ruler, any length from 6"–18" (15–45cm) long.

- Scissors for cutting paper patterns.

- Scissors reserved for cutting fabric.

- Seam ripper, just in case you mess up.

- Sewing machine that makes nice, straight stitches, zigzag stitches and button holes.

- Straight pins.

- Tape measure at least 60" (1.5m) long.

- Yardstick for drawing long lines.

vocab

appliqué A piece of fabric cut in a particular shape and then sewn onto the surface of another piece of fabric as a decoration.

basting A long, temporary stitch sewn by machine or by hand and used for different purposes. For example, two layers of fabric might be basted together just to hold them in place more securely than with pins. Also, if an edge or ruffle needs gathering, you machine sew 2 rows of basting stitches and pull the thread that's underneath (the one from the bobbin) to draw up the edge. If the instructions tell you to "baste," then you make these large stitches in the place specified. Once the project is finished, always remove any basting stitches that you can see.

bias Most project pieces are placed straight on the fabric's grain (parallel to the selvage) or cross grain (perpendicular to the selvage). Project pieces that are cut "on the bias" are placed on

CUT ON THE GRAIN

CUT ON THE BIAS

the fabric diagonally. (Explanations for grain and selvage follow.) Fabric pieces cut on the bias fall into prettier, softer folds or wrap smoother around the body.

bias binding A long strip of narrow fabric with folded edges that's used for different purposes. For example, you can stitch one long edge of a binding along your project and then fold the binding to the wrong side. When you stitch the other edge, the strip of fabric becomes a casing or a neat finish for the edge.

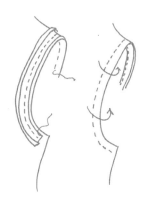

casing A tunnel that's made from two layers of fabric. You use it to hold a drawstring or elastic.

drawstring A ribbon or cord that's inserted through a casing. You pull, and then tie, the drawstring to tighten or close an edge.

CASING

fabric grain or grainline The direction of the threads in the fabric you are using. Believe it or not, it makes a big difference with your finished project if you cut the project pieces according to the fabric grain called for in the instructions or by the arrow shown on pattern pieces you'd buy at the store. Most project pieces are cut with the side edges parallel to the selvage or **on the grain**. In other cases, you need to cut the pieces with the side edges perpendicular to the selvage or **across the grain**. Always follow your project instructions regarding the grain.

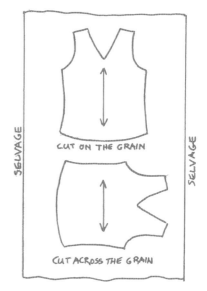

SELVAGE

CUT ON THE GRAIN

SELVAGE

CUT ACROSS THE GRAIN

flat felled seam A special way to sew a seam so that it's strong and flat. Look at the thick seams on your jeans, at the inseams along the inside of your legs. In most jeans, these are flat felled. After you sew a seam, you trim away one seam allowance and wrap the other seam allowance around this shorter side. Then it's topstitched through all the layers.

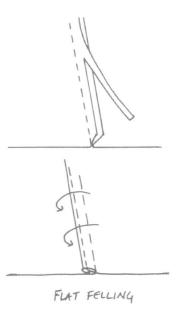

FLAT FELLING

gusset A strip or triangular piece of fabric that's inserted in the side between a front and back of something. It's generally used to expand the space inside of an item and give it more room. Although there are different types of gussets, in this book it refers to the side pieces of a bag that pull apart so you can open the bag wider.

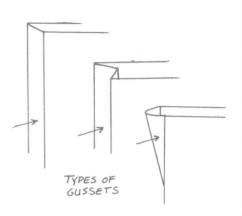

TYPES OF GUSSETS

inseam The seam on the inside of a pant leg. Some pant sizes are based on the length of the inseam.

interfacing Special material that you sew or fuse on the back of some fabric pieces to make them crisper, stiffer and stronger. Collars, hats, purses, and waistbands usually need interfacing.

remnant A piece of fabric from the end of a roll or bolt. A remnant can be anywhere from ⅛ yard–3 yards (.11m–2.73m) long. In sewing stores, you'll find remnants rolled into bundles and sold together in a mixed variety. Sometimes the prices are marked lower than usual.

ribbing A stretch fabric with vertical texture. It's usually used to finish edges like necklines, sleeves, and some-times hems on sweaters, T-shirts and sweatshirts.

RIBBING

right side and wrong side The right side of the fab-ric is the pretty side that you see when your project is finished. The wrong side is the back of the right side. The wrong side usually isn't as bright or as pretty. If you really can't tell the difference, which happens sometimes, just pick one side of the fabric and pretend you can.

seam allowance The distance between the cut edge of the fabric piece and the place where you're supposed to stitch, parallel to the cut edge. The projects in this book, and any other project instructions, will tell you the seam allowance width that you need to use for the project. To make it easier to sew straight and accurately, sewing machines have little guidelines grooved into a metal plate, called the **throat plate**, to the right of the needle area. These grooves show different distances from the needle. Get out your tape measure or ruler and find the line on the throat plate that matches your pattern's seam allowance width. If the throat plate doesn't have lines, or the lines are in metric and your pattern is in inches, create your own guide by sticking a piece of masking tape the correct distance from the needle. Line up the raw edge of your fabric with the correct line or tape edge and stitch away.

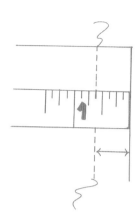

selvage The tight edge along two parallel sides of the fabric. A selvage doesn't unravel. Sometimes it has writing, blocks of color, or no color at all on it. Some selvages are ½" (1.3cm) wide and others are wider. Even though this edge is nice and neat, it's not a good idea to include it in any part of your project because it doesn't hang or wash like the rest of the fabric. In other words, trim it away.

skein A unit used for selling yarn and embroidery floss. A skein is often wound or woven into a ball, oblong or coiled shape.

staystitching A helper stitch that isn't used for major seaming. In a number of projects in this book, staystitching is used to hold layers together so they don't slide around when you stitch the final seam. Normally, you staystitch a bit closer to the fabric edge than the seam allowance for that project so that the stitch is hidden in the seam allowance once the project is finished.

tacking Hand or machine stitching used to attach two or more layers together in one spot.

topstitching Machine stitching that you see on the outside of the finished project.

do you measure up?

Take a good look at your tape measure and get clear about the markings.

- $\frac{1}{2}''$ Each inch is split in half with a long mark. There are two sections to each inch.

- $\frac{1}{4}''$ Those half-inch sections are split in half again with a shorter mark. There are four sections to each inch.

- $\frac{1}{8}''$ Quarter sections are split again with the shortest mark. There are eight sections to each inch.

1 yard = 36"	¾ yard = 27"
¼ yard = 9"	⅞ yard = 31½"
⅜ yard = 13½"	1 meter = 100 centimeters
½ yard = 18"	1 centimeter = 10 millimeters
⅝ yard = 22½"	

taking your measurements

Unless mentioned otherwise, all the projects in this book are based on your measurements and not on the size you wear in clothes you buy off the rack. In the true style of *haute couture*, you will cut and fit everything especially for you.

Grab your tape measure and take measurements for the bust, waist, hips and a few more areas. If you have trouble wrapping the tape around your body evenly, get a friend to help. When you start a project, you'll need to write down the lengths that you get when you measure around the following places: around the head, over the bust, bust, waist, hips.

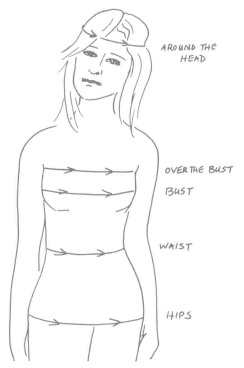

AROUND THE HEAD

OVER THE BUST

BUST

WAIST

HIPS

shopping for fabrics

If you love to go shopping for clothes and accessories, imagine going to a sewing store where everything in the shop has the potential to become an original creation. Included in the shopping list for each project in this book, you'll find suggestions for the types of fabric that are best suited for making the project. But you can adapt the design to other materials if you want. As you weigh your choices, think about what would work best.

Before you buy fabric, take a good look at it. Try to envision it made up into your project. Consider if the project requires fabric that is stiff or soft, firm or flowing, stretchy, or sheer.

Consider how wide the fabric is on the bolt. You want to buy fabric that's wide enough for the project pieces that you'll cut from it. Project instructions tell you the width that you'll need. Don't buy fabric that's too narrow unless the project instructions come with tips on how to piece (sew together) extra fabric side-by-side to make it wider, when necessary. Consider if a print works in the direction you'll be cutting the fabric. Think about how you'll need to wash or clean the project once you're done. Look at the end of the fabric bolt for care instructions or get advice from a store clerk.

Before you start your project, preshrink the fabric according to the instructions by washing, drying or steaming with the iron depending on the type of fabric you selected. Use the same settings on the washer, dryer or iron that you would use for the finished project.

sewing techniques

There is more to sewing than stitching a straight line. Depending on your project, you may have special challenges with knits, buttonholes and sewing around corners. For successful results, check out these helpful hints before you get started.

finishing raw edges When it comes to sewing, one detail separates the experts from the wannabes. The pros tidy and secure the inside raw fabric edges (called finishing) as they go along. The wannabes take the lazy route and leave the edges raw. Of course, they unravel after a few rounds in the washing machine. If you work hard to make your own stuff, you'll want it to look as good on the inside as it does on the outside, right? This isn't going to take a lot of extra effort because you only need to finish the edges that you'll see—places like seams. Don't worry about edges that are turned in and hidden, such as hems.

From here on out you can decide for yourself to finish or not to finish raw fabric edges. You'll find the instructions mention a little something about finishing off the edges, but that's just to remind you when it's a good idea to do so. If you opt to take the extra step for finishing, there are a number of ways that you can handle the raw edges. Choose from the following:

- **serger stitching** Notice this loopy (overlock) stitch inside the clothes you buy in stores.

Generally, you need a special machine for this effect, but some sewing machines have stitches that substitute for serger stitching.

- **zigzag stitching** Use an average sewing machine set to sew with a wide and long stitch.

The needle swings from side to side as the fabric moves through the sewing machine in the usual manner, from back to front. Make the zigzag stitch right along the raw edge.

- **hemming** Turn under the very edge of the fabric and sew it to create a very narrow hem.

- **pinking** Trim the seam allowances with special "pinking" scissors to cut a jagged edge.

stitching knits Knits and fabrics with stretch are easy to sew if you follow some simple rules:

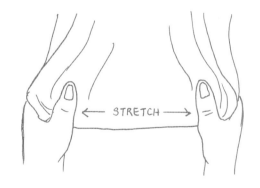

1. Gently pull your fabric from top to bottom or side to side to see which direction has the most stretch. Cut

your project pieces with the most stretch going around the body.

2. Sew knits with stretch or zigzag stitching. If the fabric stretches and the stitching doesn't, the threads will break.

• **straight stretch stitching** Two stitches forward and one stitch back. Each backstitch gives a little stretch if the stitch is yanked.

• **small zigzag stitching** Stitches sewn side to side, which means there's built-in flexibility for stretching.

3. Use a ball point or universal point needle in your sewing machine.

4. If the stretch fabric is loosely knit, finish the cut edges of the seam allowance to prevent runs in the fabric.

5. If any seam or hem stretches out of shape while you're sewing it, place the item flat on your ironing board. Lightly restore the shape by hand and then press or steam it with an iron.

sewing and pressing polar-type fleece Polar-type fleece is a knit and stretches across the grain. However, in many cases including the hat and pompom boa included in this book, you can sew fleece with an ordinary straight stitch on your sewing machine. Set the machine to sew a medium to long stitch. If you happened to make a mistake, ripping out small stitches on fleece is a real pain. The raw edges on fleece don't unravel so you won't have to finish the seam allowances with a zigzagging or serging stitch. You might want to trim the seam allowances to reduce bulkiness.

Polar-type fleece needs almost no pressing. Never touch fleece with a hot iron because it could ruin or melt the soft surface. If you need to encourage a seam to stay flat or open, set the iron for medium steam and only hold it *over* the fleece. Let the steam shoot down into the fibers. Then pat the area with your hand. Use your judgment with the hot steam and don't burn yourself.

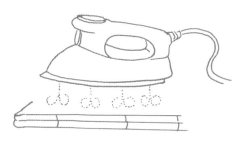

pivoting corners In order to stitch around a corner in a neat, continuous way, follow a few easy steps:

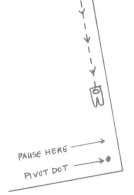

1. Begin by marking a dot with your disappearing pencil at the corner where the stitch lines (not the cut edges) come together.

2. When you're stitching the leading edge, PAUSE at about ½" (1.3cm) from the dot.

3. Turn the hand wheel on the sewing machine toward you a few times until the needle goes all the way down in the fabric directly on the dot and STOP.

PAUSE HERE

PIVOT DOT

4. Lift up the presser foot on the sewing machine. The fabric should be held in place by the needle that's still in the down position.

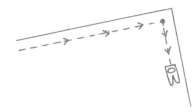

5. Shift the fabric so that the next side is rotated in place for stitching. Lower the presser foot and you're good to go.

mitering corners In many projects, you'll need to turn under the edge of the fabric and stitch a hem along 2 or more sides. In order to hem around the corners neatly, you fold the fabric in the corner at a diagonal before turning it under to make a miter.

1. Beginning on the first side, fold under the raw edge and fold again on the final hem line. Stitch close to the inside fold nearly the full length of the first side. At a distance from the corner about twice the width of the hem allowance, PAUSE and lower the sewing machine needle down into the fabric, holding the hem in place.

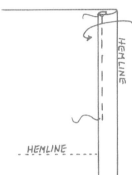

2. Fold the corner hem allowance over diagonally.

3. On the next side, fold under the raw edge the same way as on the first side.

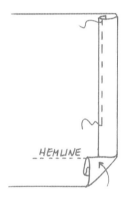

4. Fold again on the hemline, making a sharp corner with the hem allowance turned under diagonally. Turn the hand wheel on the sewing machine toward you a few times, manually stitching beyond the hem allowance on the first side until the needle goes into the hem edge on the next side. Stop at this point. Lift up the presser foot on the sewing machine. The hem on the second side should be held in place by the needle that's still in the down position. Shift the fabric so that the next side is rotated in place for stitching. Lower the presser foot and continue hemming.

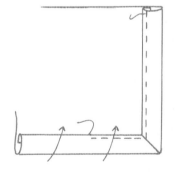

inserting buttonholes Every sewing machine has a unique way to make buttonholes, but basically, the steps are the same for all of them. You make buttonholes with a combination of wide and medium zigzag stitches that are sewn very tightly together.

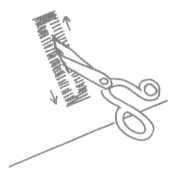

Whether your machine makes a buttonhole automatically or with a series of individual steps, brief yourself on what you have to do. Start by marking the buttonhole on the right side of the fabric with your dressmaker pencil. Set the machine stitch length on a buttonhole setting or

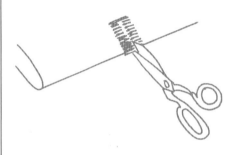

very close together (satin stitch). Set the stitch width at half of the maximum. Sew along the right-hand side the full length of the buttonhole. Then change the stitch width to the maximum setting and sew a few stitches. Change the stitch width back to the half setting and stitch back along the left-hand side before completing the buttonhole with a wide stitch at the starting point.

A good way to cut open a buttonhole is to fold it in half and snip from the center with sharp scissors. Unfold and finish cutting the center of the buttonhole to each end.

icon key

Icons identify terms for sewing functions that often appear in sewing instructions. If you see an icon in the text that you don't understand, flip back to this page for a translation.

backtack At the beginning of your stitching—and again at the end of your stitching—sew forward one or two stitches, sew backward a few stitches, and then sew forward again. This knots the start and end of your seam line.

clip and notch seam allowances Cut little slits or Vs into the seam allowance around a curved section or wherever noted.

Clip slits on curves that go in and Vs on curves that go out. Cutting Vs is called notching. Don't confuse notching with notches, which are those little diamond shapes that may appear on the edge of sewing patterns.

cut, crop, or trim Just what it says. Cut along the line or wherever it says to do so in the instructions.

fuse Use an iron to join two fabric layers or a layer of fabric and a layer of interfacing together with special glue that's activated by heat or steam. Fusible interfacing, patches and appliqués come with the glue already sprayed on the back. Read the directions from the manufacturer to see how to fuse the interfacing or fusible tape correctly.

match marks or notches

Line up the marks you made with a pencil or pin or the notches that you'll find on commercial patterns. When you have a notch, it usually matches another notch on an opposite side or a joining fabric piece.

press, iron, or steam

Iron everything flat and smooth or else hold the iron just a bit above the fabric and give it a shot of steam. The instructions will tell you whether you need to "iron" or "steam" your fabric.

press the seam allowances open

Spread the seam allowances apart and iron or finger-press right down the middle of the opening, along the seam line.

right sides together

Place the fabric pieces together so that the pretty sides are facing each other.

seam allowances

The fabric between the cut edge and the place where you're supposed to stitch.

turn the right sides out

Pull the outer side of your project through any available opening so that the pretty side of the fabric is on the outside.

a few reminders

Read everything carefully before you start. Believe me, this cuts down on mistakes—and we all know what a drag it is to tear out stitches and do things over again.

Each set of project instructions will tell you what seam allowance to use for that project. Although with apparel sewing patterns you usually use ⅝" (15mm) seam allowances, many garment projects in this book call for ½" (13mm) seam allowances for ease in converting and calculating measurements. In all cases, check the instructions before you start to sew.

Always pull your pins out along the way when you're sewing. Never stitch over pins. You can break sewing machine needles and mess up your machine.

At the beginning and end of each seam, backtack your stitches to knot the seam, unless the instructions tell you not to do so.

When your project is finished, remove any marks from the dressmaker pencil that are still visible. Use the method that works for the type of pencil you have according to the manufacturer's directions.

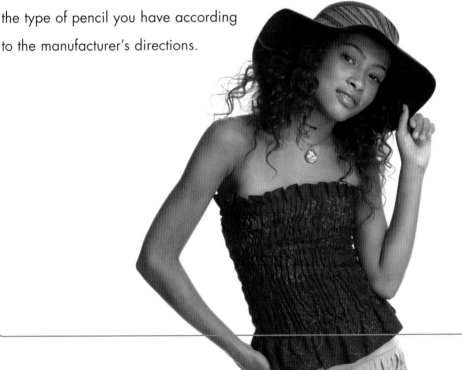

skirts

scarf skirt

tiered eyelet skirt

patchwork skirt

stitch & slash mini

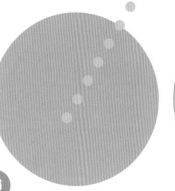

crinkled prairie skirt

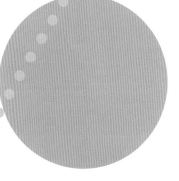

Comfy and uniquely feminine, skirts soften the edges in any girl's wardrobe. Choose a style that reflects the real you and give those tired jeans a rest.

crinkled prairie skirt
how-to's on pg. 54

What happens when you layer a square of chiffon on top of a square of crepe fabric? With minimal effort, a fun and flirty skirt appears in no time. Slip it on. Twirl around. Such a skirt may conjure up long forgotten memories of playing in your mother's scarf drawer, only this time, your imaginary skirt is real.

scarf skirt

scarf skirt

Start by grabbing your tape measure and taking your measurements. Flip back to page 16 for details. Fill in measurements and equations on the blanks provided for ease in figuring out the size of cut fabric pieces. Follow the labels at each blank to help identify your calculations.

Waist measurement + 1" (2.5cm) = A._____

Hip measurement = B._____

shopping list

- 2 coordinating scarf-weight fabrics—each as long as the width of the narrowest fabric.

- 1 pack of single-fold bias binding to match the top fabric, ½" (13mm) wide.

- Elastic, ¼" (6mm) wide, long enough to match measurement A.

- Thread to match the fabric.

You make the skirt by layering 2 coordinating scarf-weight fabrics in a print or solid. One fabric can be sheer (or slightly see-through), such as chiffon. One fabric must be opaque (not see-through), such as crepe, crinkle crepe or blouse-weight satin. While shopping for supplies, open up the fabric choices and place one layer over another to see how they look together.

The width of the fabric is important because it determines the amount of yardage you need to buy, and also affects the length of the finished skirt. Once you've found fabrics that you can't live without, look to see which one of the two is the narrowest from selvage to selvage. Round up this smaller number to the nearest ½ yard (or meter, if you're working in metric). For example, if one fabric is 44" (115cm) wide and the other is 60" (150cm) wide, the narrowest is 44" (115cm) or approximately 1¼ yards (1.14m). Round this amount up to 1½ yards (1.37m). You'll need to get 1½ yards (1.37m) of each fabric.

scarf skirt

Believe it or not, sometimes you can rip your fabric instead of cutting it. The fiber content, weave, and weight of the fabric is the determining factor. Cut a little slit along one edge, firmly grip each side of the slit and quickly pull. This works well with soft, lightweight fabric such as crepe or scarf-weight broadcloth. First try ripping off a bit of the selvage. If the threads are pulling and not ripping neatly, you either aren't pulling sharply enough or the fabric isn't suitable for ripping.

So why in the world would you rip your fabric? Actually, it makes a perfect edge along the straight grain or cross grain of the fabric. For skirts, scarves or anything with edges that need to be completely accurate, it works like a charm.

cutting

Cut or rip 2 equal squares, as large as possible, 1 from each fabric. For best results, all 4 edges of your squares must be cut accurately along the straight grain and cross grain.

Start by cutting or ripping a square from the narrowest fabric. Straighten one cut edge evenly along the thread line for the cross grain. If it's hard to see the threads in your fabric or it doesn't rip neatly, cut a little slit through the selvage. Find a single thread and gently pull it to make a guideline. Cut along the thread guideline until you can't see the pulled thread any longer. Find another thread and pull it in the same way. Repeat this little by little until

you've trimmed the fabric completely along the cross grain.

In the same manner, trim the selvage off of the 2 side edges of each fabric square. Measure the first cut edge along the cross grain. This can be called Measurement C. Find the length of Measurement C along the side edges (previously the selvage) to figure out the final cut (see diagram). Trim the last edge to make a perfect square. Repeat this for both of the fabric squares.

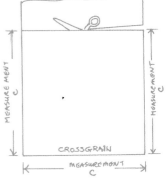

MEASUREMENT C

MEASUREMENT C

CROSSGRAIN

MEASUREMENT C

sewing

Each fabric square is one layer of the finished skirt. Starting at the corner of one layer, fold and press ¼" (6mm) of the raw fabric edge to the wrong side, then fold up another ¼" (6mm) to the wrong side, so that the first fold is sandwiched inside. Topstitch along the inside fold of the first edge. When you come to the corner, miter the hem allowance (see page 21). Hem all 4 of the edges on both squares in this same way.

Press the hem edges nice and flat.

Calculate the size of the skirt opening by using the following chart. Find the number in the first column equal to Measurement B and look for the radius for marking the cut line.

hip measurement	skirt opening radius
Up to 28" (71.1cm)	4½" (11.4cm)
28½" to 31" (72.3–78.7cm)	5" (12.7cm)
31½" to 34" (80–86.4cm)	5½" (14cm)
34½" to 37½" (87.6–95.3cm)	6" (15.2cm)
38" to 41" (96.5–104.1cm)	6½" (16.5cm)
41½" to 44" (105.4–111.8cm)	7" (17.8cm)
44½" to 47" (113–119.4cm)	7½" (19cm)
47½" to 50" (120.7–127cm)	8" (20.3cm)

scarf skirt

Decide which square you want to use as the top layer and which will be on the bottom. Fold the top layer into quarters and place it on a tabletop in a neat square. If you need to, pin all of the layers together at the edges to keep them from shifting. From the folded corner, measure out the radius you got from the table and, with a tape measure, use your dressmaker pencil to mark this on the top layer of the fabric square. Measure and mark the radius several times, at different spots, to make a complete curve that's always the same distance from the folded corner (see top diagram). Draw a notch at each folded edge. Cut 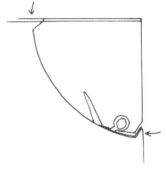 the notches and the opening along this line (see bottom diagram).

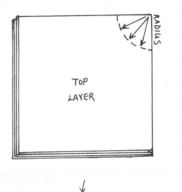

Fold the remaining fabric square (the bottom layer of the skirt) in half diagonally, and then in half again. Place this neat triangle on a tabletop. Pin through all of the layers (this fabric layer hasn't been pinned before) to keep the edges together. Repeat the same process, measuring and marking the notches and cutting line using the radius you figured out in the last step (see diagram). Cut the notches and the opening along this line.

Unfold the layers. With the right sides facing up, place the top layer over the bottom layer, matching the notches 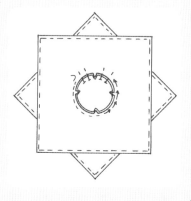 and the cut edges of the opening. Pin the layers together around the opening. Staystitch the layers together, no more than ¼" (6mm) from the edges of the opening (see diagram).

Open one long, folded side of the bias binding and then fold ½" (1.3cm) on a short end to the wrong side. Place the end fold at any notch with the long, raw edge of the bias binding aligned with the raw edges of the opening and with right sides together 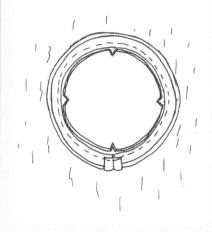. Stitch the binding around the opening edge by sewing in the fold on the open side with ¼" (6mm) seam allowance . When you're all the way around to the beginning of the bias binding, fold the final end under so that the 2 folds butt together at the beginning and end. Don't sew the bind-ing ends together because you'll need to leave an opening for insert-ing the elastic later (see diagram).

Along the seam you just made, fold the binding under to the inside of the skirt and press . Topstitch the opposite edge of the binding, still folded, through all of the skirt layers to make a casing. Insert a safety pin through an end of the elastic. Insert the pin through the opening where the binding ends join, and then thread the elastic through the casing. Try on the skirt. With it still on you, pull the elastic tight enough to feel comfortable around the waist or off the waist, wherever you want it to sit on your body. Pin the elastic together where you want them joined. Take off the skirt. Check to make sure the elastic isn't twisted in the casing. Overlap the elastic ends and stitch them together.

Soft and feminine, an eyelet skirt with gathered tiers is a classic. Every girl should have a skirt like this hanging in her closet. Look for fabric with a pretty bordered scallop along one edge.

tiered eyelet skirt

tiered eyelet skirt

project calculations

Start by grabbing your tape measure and taking your measurements. Flip back to page 16 for details. Fill in measurements and equations on the blanks provided for ease in figuring out the size of cut fabric pieces. Follow the labels at each blank to help identify your calculations.

In order to use the calculator to figure out a number based on a percentage, start by punching in the original number. In the first case this is Measurement A. Push the addition symbol (+). Click on the percentage number, in this case 70. Now, push the percent symbol (%). If you get an uneven number—and in most cases you will—round it up to the nearest whole number. Write this number in the blank for Measurement B.

Repeat the process to calculate Measurement C.

Hip measurement + 2" (5cm) = A._____

Measurement A + 70% = B._____

Measurement B + 70% = C._____

Measurement A x 2 =   D._____

Waist measurement + ½" (1.3cm) = E._____

shopping list

- Eyelet fabric with a scallop border, 44" (115cm) wide or more: enough yardage to equal Measurement C plus another complete scallop.

- Lining fabric to match the eyelet fabric, 44" (115cm) wide or more: enough yardage to equal Measurement D.

- Elastic, ¾" (19mm) wide: enough yardage to equal Measurement E.

- Thread to match the fabric.

tiered eyelet skirt

cutting

Cut all parts of the skirt and lining, as explained below, "across the grain" with the long edges parallel to the selvage and scalloped edge (see diagram 1).

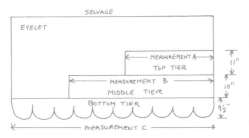

diagram 1

The skirt has 3 tiers. From the deepest part of a scallop, measure 9½" (24.1cm) into the eyelet fabric and cut the entire length of the fabric at this depth, for the bottom tier.

At each short end of the bottom tier, place a pin at the shallowest part in the scallop and draw a line ½" (13cm) out from the pin, for the seam allowance (see diagram 2). Trim along these two lines, to cut off the excess scallop at both ends.

Turning again to the eyelet fabric yardage, from the long edge that you cut for the bottom tier, measure 10" (25.4cm) farther into the fabric. Using this depth for the middle tier, cut the length to equal Measurement B.

From the cut edge, measure 11" (27.9cm) farther into the fabric and cut the top tier. Trim the length to equal Measurement A (see diagram 1).

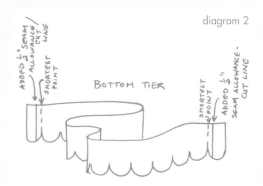

diagram 2

The lining has 2 tiers. Starting along one selvage edge (don't forget to trim the selvage off), cut a lining piece 18½" (47cm) wide and as long as Measurement D for the bottom lining tier.

Cut 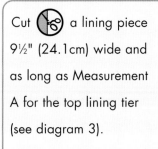 a lining piece 9½" (24.1cm) wide and as long as Measurement A for the top lining tier (see diagram 3).

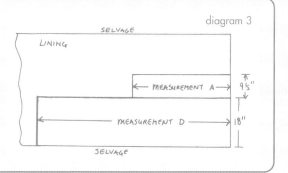

diagram 3

SELVAGE

LINING

MEASUREMENT A

9⅕"

MEASUREMENT D

18"

SELVAGE

sewing

Use a ½" (13mm) seam allowance unless mentioned otherwise. Finish the seam allowances however you like, with zigzag or serger stitching (see page 18 for a description of these choices).

Making sure that the fabric length isn't twisted and with the right sides together , match the short ends of the top eyelet tier and stitch. The tier is now a circle. Repeat the same step for each of the remaining eyelet and lining tiers. Since you're using ½" (13mm) seam allowance, the bottom tier will be seamed at the shortest point in the scallop at each short end. (Isn't that pretty when you go to a little extra trouble?)

Press the seam allowances open for all of the tiers.

In this step, you're working on the eyelet fabric tiers. Fold the top tier into quarters and place a tiny mark at each fold, along the bottom edge, with the disappearing pencil. In the same way, fold the middle tier, but mark both the top and bottom of the folds. Repeat with the bottom tier, but mark only the top folds (see diagram). Once the edges are gathered, the marks make it easy to match the edges of the tiers.

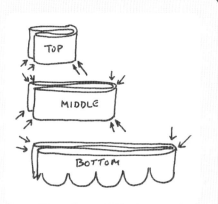

TOP

MIDDLE

BOTTOM

tiered eyelet skirt

Starting with the middle tier of the eyelet fabric, machine sew a basting stitch that's ⅜" (10mm) from the top edge. Sew another basting stitch ⅝" (15mm) from the top edge. In both cases, don't backtack or overlap the beginning and end of the stitching line and leave long threads at each end. With right sides together 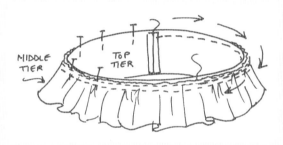, pin this basted edge to the bottom (unstitched) edge of the top tier by matching the seam lines and the pencil marks. The middle tier will be much longer than the top tier. Gently pull the bobbin threads on the basting stitches to gather up the longer edge to fit the top tier. Spread the gathers out evenly and pin the edges together. Stitch between the two lines of basting stitches, around the entire pinned edge. When you do this, don't forget to switch your sewing machine back to a shorter stitch length (see diagram).

Sew 2 rows of basting stitches, one ⅜" (10mm) and another ⅝" (15mm), from the top edge of the bottom tier of the eyelet fabric. In the same manner as the last step, pin the bottom eyelet tier to the middle tier, gathering the edge to fit and then stitching the edges together (see diagram).

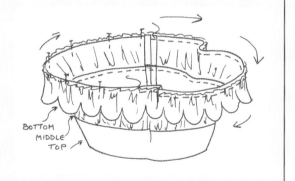

Mark the bottom edge of the top lining tier and the top edge of the bottom lining tier in the same way as the outside of the skirt (the eyelet fabric). Sew 2 lines of basting stitches along the top edge of the bottom tier. With right sides together 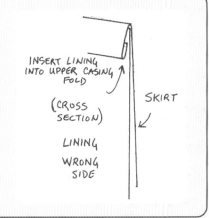, pin the bottom lining tier to the top lining tier. Gather and stitch the edges in the same manner as before. Pull out all the basting stitches on all the skirt and lining tiers.

Along the opposite raw edge of the bottom lining tier, press under ¾" (1.9cm) and then press under another ¾" (1.9cm). Topstitch this doubled hem around the lining. Press it again (see diagram).

At the top of the top tier of the eyelet layer, press under ½" (1.3cm) and then another 1" (2.5cm) to make a casing around the top edge. Place the right side of the lining next to the wrong side of the skirt. Line up the center back seam lines and slide the top edge of the lining into the outside casing fold (see diagram). Pin the casing down to hold the lining in place. Topstitch along the first casing fold, leaving a 1" (2.5cm) opening at the seam.

INSERT LINING INTO UPPER CASING FOLD

(CROSS SECTION)

SKIRT

LINING WRONG SIDE

Attach a safety pin to an end of the elastic. Insert the pin into the casing opening and thread it completely through the casing. Overlap the elastic ends and stitch them together. Stitch the skirt casing opening closed. Now you'll have to treat yourself to a pretty little top to wear with this skirt.

If vintage is your thing, mix it up with patches, prints, and a traditional semi-circle skirt that even your grandmother will appreciate. Raid the remnant bin or dig out your favorite scraps for piecing inspiration.

patchwork skirt

patchwork skirt

project calculations

Start by grabbing your tape measure and taking your measurements. Flip back to page 16 for details. Fill in measurements and equations on the blanks provided for ease in figuring out the size of the cut fabric pieces. Follow the labels at each blank to help identify your calculations.

Follow the quantities provided here for a knee-length skirt (and in parentheses for mid-calf and ankle-length). All lengths are approximate. Add extra squares for a longer or wider panel.

Hip measurement + ½" (1.3cm) = A._____

Measurement from the waist (or hip), taken along the side of the body, to the desired finished length + 1" = B._____

shopping list

Pick out 10 or more different fabrics, 44" wide or wider, that look good together and suit your taste. Groups of fabrics should be the same weight and similar quality.

- Fabrics 44"–45" wide—⅜ (⅝, ¾) yard from each.
- 1 pack of extra wide, single fold bias binding.
- ½" (13mm) wide elastic, 15" long.
- Optional: Beads, bells, charms, or tassels to hang from the tie ends.
- Thread to match the fabric.

you'll also need...

- A piece of tagboard or old cereal box (cut open so it's flat), for the patch pattern.

patchwork skirt

making a pattern

Cut a 5" (12.7cm) square for a patch pattern from the tagboard.

cutting

From the fabric assortment, use the patch pattern to cut 128 (242, 392) square patches. Although you may use any quantity you like, it's easier to arrange the patches when you have the same number from each fabric. Cut a 2" (5cm) strip of any one fabric the full width from selvage to selvage. This is for the tie.

sewing

Use ¼" (6mm) seam allowance unless mentioned otherwise.

Lay out rows of patches in a random arrangement or repeating pattern. If you like the repeating pattern, make sure you have enough patches to completely finish sewing the squares together. Arrange vertical rows, each with 8 (11, 14) patches. Try to plan the rows so that the top patches at one end are contrasting from the corresponding patches at the other end. Plan 16 (22, 28) vertical rows altogether.

Starting with the first row, stitch two patches along one edge with right sides together. Finish off the seam allowances with zigzag or serging stitches. Now sew another patch to the joined ones. Continue adding more patches to make a vertical row of seamed patches (see diagram). Once you've completed rows in the order you like, number the rows with a little label to keep track of which row goes where (see diagram).

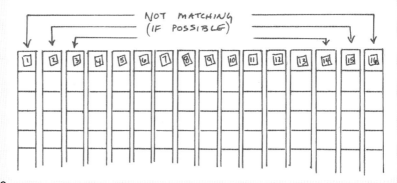

Seam the rows together in the order that you've set up. Finish off the seam allowances in the same way you did when you made the rows. Press the pieced fabric nice and flat.

Fold the fabric in half with the short ends and right sides together. At the top, place a mark along the fold line ¼" (.6cm) from the corner, to represent the stitch line. Now you are going to calculate the size of the skirt opening. In the following chart, find your Measurement A, which you determined in the Project Calculations, and look across to find your radius for marking the cut line.

measurement A	radius
Up to 31" (78.7cm)	10" (25.4cm)
31¼" to 32½" (82.6cm)	10½" (26.7cm)
32¾" to 34" (86.4cm)	11" (27.9cm)
34¼" to 36" (91.4cm)	11½" (29.2cm)
36¼" to 37½" (95cm)	12" (30.5cm)
37¾" to 39" (99.1cm)	12½" (31.8cm)
39¼" to 40½" (102.9cm)	13" (33cm)
40¾" to 42" (106.7cm)	13½" (34.3cm)
42¼" to 44" (111.8cm)	14" (35.6cm)
44¼" to 46" (116.8cm)	14½" (36.8cm)

patchwork skirt

Measure out from the corner mark the length of the correct radius. Mark several points to make an arc for the waist cutting line (see diagram 1). Cut 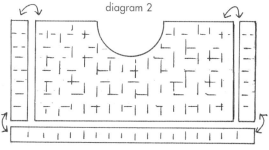 on this line through both layers. Hold the waist cutting line edge up to your waist or lower on the hips—wherever you'd like to wear your skirt—to see if the fabric is long enough for the look you want based on the shortest length found in the center. To lengthen, piece together and add extra rows of patches to the remaining three sides (see diagram 2).

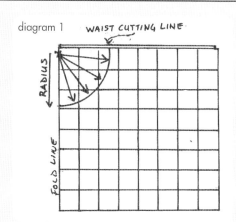

diagram 1   WAIST CUTTING LINE

RADIUS

FOLD LINE

diagram 2

Once the pieced fabric is long enough, fold it in half, again, bringing the top edges and right sides together . Stitch together the top edges and then finish the seam allowances separately (see diagram). Press the seam allowances open . Lay the skirt flat with the right side out .

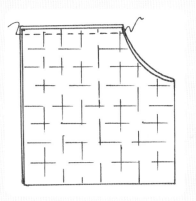

Open one fold along the length of the bias binding and fold under one short end. Starting at the open seam, with right sides together 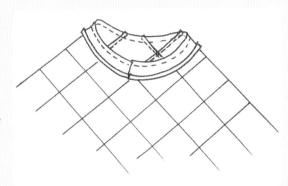, and a long cut edge of the bias binding aligned with the skirt's opening, stitch in the open fold around the waistline. Lap the opposite end of the bias binding 1" (2.5cm) over the folded end and trim off any excess binding (see diagram). Fold the binding under to the inside of the skirt along the seam line and press . Topstitch the opposite edge of the binding to the skirt, through all the layers, to make a casing. Make another line of topstitching at the top edge of the skirt, close to the folded edge (the seam line), if you like. On the outside of the skirt, at the seam that was pressed open, remove a few stitches at the casing to make an opening.

Fold the long tie strip in half lengthwise, with wrong sides together, and press . Tuck the long raw edges up into the fold and press again . Stitch the folds together along the open edge to make a tie. Cut the tie in half and stitch a raw end to each end of the elastic (see diagram). Attach the large safety pin to one end of the finished tie and thread it through the skirt casing.

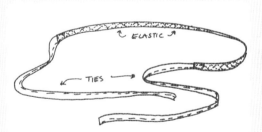

ELASTIC

TIES

patchwork skirt

Try on the skirt and place the tie at your left hip. Once you have it tied in a comfortable position, get a friend to measure down from the waist edge the length of Measurement B and mark this spot with a pin. Hold the yardstick on end and measure from the floor up to this pin. Have your friend repeat this marking process in several places around the bottom of the skirt using the floor-to-pin measurement. Don't forget that when the skirt is done, the hem allowance will make the finished length 1" (2.5cm) shorter than the pin marks. Take the skirt off and place it flat on a table. Draw a line between the pins with your dressmaker pencil. Trim off excess fabric along the line. You'll find you will have some scraps of pieced fabric. Save them for another project.

Press 1" (2.5cm) up (to the wrong side of the skirt) completely around the hem. Tuck the raw edge down into the fold and press again . Topstitch the hem in place. Press the whole skirt again if it needs it.

Add beads, bells, tassels, charms or whatever you like to the ends of the tie.

tips

If you like this design
and want to put a different spin on it, choose fabrics with a theme.

casual or trendy
Denim that's stitched with the patch seams on the outside.

elegant, bohemian, or costumey
Velvets, pannés, and soft brocades.

country or traditional
Quilting cottons and calicos.

dressy or feminine
Lightweight satins and jacquards.

Don't you wish all your clothes were as comfy as your favorite T-shirts? Your wish can come true. Cut open a couple of blank tees in coordinating colors, and then layer them together. Stitch and slash your own unique design for a skirt that's completely original.

stitch & slash mini

stitch & slash mini

cutting

Place a T-shirt flat on a table. With your yardstick and pencil, draw a line between underarm seams on each side. Cut ✂ along this line through the front and back layers to remove the sleeves and the top of the shirt (see diagram). Save the top of the T-shirt to use later.

Rearrange the bottom of the shirt so that the folds are centered along the front and back of the skirt. Cut along the back fold and open the shirt bottom out into a single layer (see diagram). Repeat the same process for the second

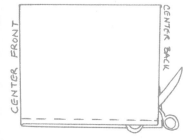

T-shirt. Leave the finished hems alone.

From the T-shirt scraps (the tops), cut ✂ 3 strips horizontally, each 3" (7.6cm) wide and as long as possible. Don't include seams or sleeves when you cut the strips. Use whatever color you want. You will sew these strips together to make one long strip for the waistband.

stitch & slash mini

planning your design

Plan a thoroughly unique stitch-and-slash design. Consider your pattern as a series of positives and negatives, or big blocks of space filled in with the two alternating colors that you picked out. In later steps, you'll layer the two T-shirt bottoms, stitch through both, and then trim 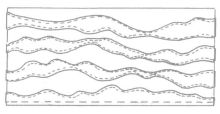 just the top layer, to reveal the bottom layer. The more you trim 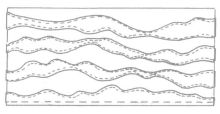, the more of the bottom layer you'll see.

Here are a few examples to give you a clearer idea about what you can do:

Closely spaced horizontal rows of stitching alternated with wide, unstitched sections that are cut 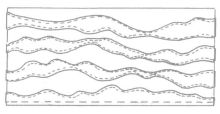 with oblong vertical holes (see diagram 1).

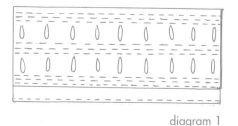

diagram 1

Horizontal rows that are stitched and cut away, alternating with wide sections that are cut into fringes (see diagram 2).

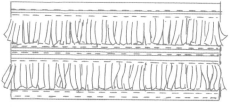

diagram 2

Freeform waves stitched horizontally from side to side with alternating spaces trimmed away 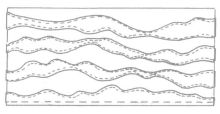 (see diagram 3).

diagram 3

Let your imagination take the lead. Grab a pencil with a good eraser and use this blank skirt shape to play with ideas for stitching designs (see diagram 4).

diagram 4

sewing

Use ½" (13mm) seam allowances 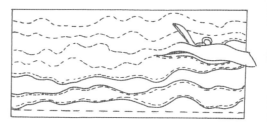 unless mentioned otherwise.

Flip back to page 18 to see tips on sewing knit fabrics that stretch.

1 Place the T-shirt panel in the top color flat on a table. With your dressmaker pencil, mark out the stitching pattern on the right side according to your personal design.

2 Lift up the top panel and place the bottom panel flat on the table, with the right side up. Layer the top panel over the bottom panel with the stitching design markings facing up. Line up the hem edges of both layers. Pin both panels together, very thoroughly, between the stitch markings and around all of the edges.

3 Sew along all the stitch design markings, through both layers. For fun, use a thread color that matches the bottom layer. This way, it will contrast with the T-shirt color in the top layer. As a rule, you should sew knit fabric with a stitch that stretches, but this T-shirt jersey will stretch slightly as you stitch your design even if you sew with an ordinary stitch. Normally this will solve the stretch problem. If your skirt is particularly tight or you like extra ease for movement, stitch with a stretch stitch. Carefully trim away the top T-shirt layer in the sections in your design, according to your plan. Be careful to only trim the top layer between stitching lines (see diagram).

stitch & slash mini

4 Fold the joined panels in half with the short edges and right sides together 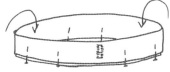. Stitch together the matched short edges to make the center back seam. Finish the seam allowances with a zigzag or serging stitch. Leave the wrong side out.

5 Sew together the waistband strips end to end, using ¼" (6mm) seam allowances ⊟. Make sure the waistband strip is long enough to fit around the top edge of the skirt. Fold the center strip in half across the width, and mark the fold with a pin. Open the fold and fuse 🔲 the interfacing square to the wrong side, at the pin, with the bottom edges aligned. At this same place, mark a vertical buttonhole, ½" (1.9 x 1.3cm) in from the bottom edge and ¾" long. Stitch the buttonhole as marked (see diagram).

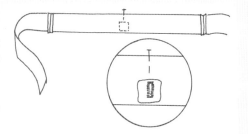

If you aren't familiar with making a buttonhole, check the operator's manual of your sewing machine. Cut ✂ the buttonhole open.

6 With right sides together 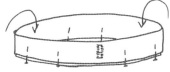, fold the waistband in half at the buttonhole. Place the waistband above the top of the skirt and pin the short ends of the waistband together to fit the same width as the skirt. Trim ✂ the excess waistband away (see top diagram). Seam the short ends of the waistband together. Refold the waistband lengthwise so that the wrong sides and raw edges are together. Pin (see bottom diagram).

Pin the waistband to the skirt with the right sides together  and the buttonhole at the center front. Stitch around the waist. Finish the seam allowances.

Cut the ribbon in half and stitch one piece to each end of the elastic. Insert the safety pin through one end of the elastic, and then use it to thread the ribbon through the buttonhole in the waistband casing. Pull the safety pin through the entire casing and out the buttonhole. Try on the skirt and tie the ribbon in a nice bow. Trim any ends that you think are too long. Tie a knot in each ribbon end if you like. You've just launched your career as a fashion designer.

Be creative! You can wear your new mini as a top *or* a skirt.

Fashion is resurrecting all those hippie styles you might find in your local second-hand store. This tiered skirt pays homage to the original bohemian look, complete with raw edges and a crinkled texture. This is also a great skirt to take on a trip. Just twist it up to pack in your suitcase and restore the crinkles at the same time.

crinkled prairie skirt

crinkled prairie skirt

project calculations

Start by grabbing your tape measure and taking your measurements. Flip back to page 16 for details. Fill in the measurements and equations on the blanks provided for ease in figuring out the size of cut fabric pieces. Follow the labels at each blank to help identify your calculations.

Waist measurement + 1" (2.5cm) = A._____

Hip measurement + 2" (5cm) = B._____

shopping list

- 5 coordinating, lightweight cotton fabrics, approximately ¾ yard (.7m) each.

- Elastic, ¾" (19mm) wide, as long as Measurement A.

- Thread to match the fabric.

you'll also need...

- Access to a washer and dryer. If you've never used these appliances before, get a quick lesson first.

cutting

Lay one of the pieces of fabric out folded in half with the selvages together. Trim 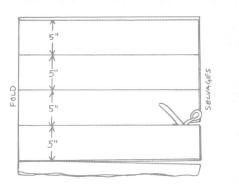 one raw edge to be perfectly perpendicular to the selvage. Starting at this edge, cut 5" (12.7cm) strips from selvage to selvage (see diagram).

crinkled prairie skirt

Trim  off the short selvage edges on each strip. With right sides together piece all the strips, end to end, using ½" (13mm) seam allowances . Finish off these short raw edges by serging or zigzagging. Repeat the same process for each of the different fabrics. You'll have 5 pieced strips of fabric altogether. These will be cut to different lengths to make the tiers for the skirt (see diagram). Each tier is a

5"
CUT SKIRT TIERS
5"

different fabric than the one above and below it. The 5" (12.7cm) strips for each tier are cut wider than the strips for the tier that will be above it on the finished skirt. In order to keep the tiers in proportion, follow this formula that's based on your own measurements. Although there is some math involved, the formula is easy if you follow the directions. Start by pulling out a calculator that has a percentage button.

Start with Measurement B. You're using the hip measurement plus 2" (5cm) extra, for ease, so that you can get your skirt on and off. This amount equals the width of tier 1, which is at the very top of the skirt.

Go ahead and fill in the first blank on the chart. Okay, now here comes the formula—let's use a 37" (94cm) hip measurement as an example. Punch Measurement B (39" or 99.1cm) in your calculator. Push the addition symbol (+). Push the number 12. Push the percent symbol (%). You'll probably get an uneven number (43.68" or 110cm). Round this number down to the nearest whole number (43" or 109cm).

Continue calculating with the tier 2 amount and the same formula. It may seem daunting, but seriously, it's not that hard. As you figure out measurements for your own skirt tiers, record them in the chart provided for easy reference.

Tier Number	Length of previous tier (column 4 number from previous row)	Length of tier in column 2 plus (+) 12%	Round number in column 3 down to nearest whole number and cut tier to this length	Use fabric listed here
column 1	column 2	column 3	column 4	column 5
example tier 1			39" (99.1cm)	A
example tier 2	39" (99cm)	43.68" (110cm)	43" (109cm)	B
example tier 3	43" (109cm)	48.16" (122cm)	48" (121cm)	C
1			your measurement B	A
2				B
3				C
4				D
5				E
6				A
7				B
8				C
9				D
10				E

Lay out your strips and play around with them, to decide the order that you want to arrange them for the skirt tiers. This is where you play fashion designer. Once you're happy with the order, pin a little paper label with "A" to the top layer, followed by "B", "C" and so on for the remaining fabric strips.

Now it's time to cut the fabric strips into the skirt tiers. Follow the measurements determined in column 4 of the table above for each tier.

Fabric A: Cut tiers 1 and 6.

Fabric B: Cut tiers 2 and 7.

Fabric C: Cut tiers 3 and 8.

Fabric D: Cut tiers 4 and 9.

Fabric E: Cut tiers 5 and 10.

crinkled prairie skirt

sewing

Use ½" seam allowances .

Starting with tier 1, fold the strip in half, bringing the short ends together.
Along the bottom raw edge, mark the fold with a
pin or a mark from a dressmaker pencil. Fold the
strip again to divide it into quarters (not counting
the seam allowances) and mark these points (see
diagram 1).

diagram 1

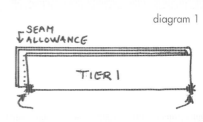

Make the same marks on tier 2,
only this time, mark both edges at the
quarter points (see diagram 2).

diagram 2

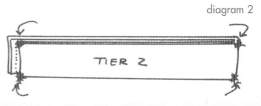

2 Open tier 1 and tier 2. With the wrong sides and raw edges together, pin the two
tiers, matching the quarter points (see diagram). (Don't forget that tier 2 is wider than
tier 1. Tier 2 will
look saggy
between the pins,

but that's okay.) Beginning at a short end, start stitching the edges together, gently
scrunching in the extra fullness and taking tiny tucks along the edge of tier 2 so that it
fits tier 1. Work on each section between the pins, and then sew the 2 tiers completely
to each other. Do not finish these raw edges with serging or zigzag stitching.

3 Fold tier 3 into quarters in the same way you worked on tiers 1 and 2. Mark the quarter points along both long edges of tier 3. Pin tiers 2 and 3 together, matching the quarter marks and raw long edges. Don't forget that the raw edges are on the outside, which means you'll have to place wrong sides together. Stitch the edges together, tucking and scrunching the fullness on tier 3 to fit to tier 2, just like before.

4 Fold tier 4 into quarters and mark the folds along one edge. Fold again to make eighths, and mark a point on the opposite edge at each newest fold. With the wrong sides and raw edges together, stitch tier 3 to tier 4, matching the quarter marks. Fold tiers 5–9 into eighths and mark both edges at each fold. Join the tiers together in the correct order and in the same way that you've been doing in the previous steps. Fold tier 10 into eighths and mark only one side. Join this edge to the bottom edge of tier 9 to complete joining the tiers.

5 Press (iron icon) all of the seam allowances down toward the hem. Fold the skirt in half lengthwise with right sides together (icon) and the tiers matching. Stitch the side edges together to make the center back seam. Press the seam allowances open (icon).

6 Press (iron icon) the top edge (tier 1) under ½" (1.3cm) and again 1" (2.5cm), to the wrong side. Stitch along the first fold to make a casing, leaving a small opening at the center back seam for the elastic.

7 Press (iron icon) the bottom edge (tier 10) up 1" (2.5cm) to the wrong side. Topstitch around the entire skirt bottom, ¼" (6mm) from the fold, to make a small tuck around the bottom hem. Press (iron icon) the raw edge down so that you can see it from beneath the tuck.

crinkled prairie skirt

Now comes the fun part. Throw the skirt in the washing machine. Run a wash cycle with cold water and little (or no) laundry detergent. If you've never used the washer before, get someone to help you. After the wash cycle is finished, take the skirt out and you'll no doubt find all the threads from the raw edges coming loose and tangled together. Just cut off ✂ any long threads. Remember, you want the edges to be unraveled. Repeat the washing process again, and trim off ✂ more long threads.

If you want the raw edges to fluff up, throw the skirt in the dryer. Once the skirt looks like it's all broken in, insert the large safety pin through one end of the elastic. Thread the elastic, pin first, through the opening and through the casing. Overlap the ends and then stitch them together.

Completely wet the skirt again. Twist it to wring out any dripping water. Keep twisting the skirt until it won't twist anymore (see diagram). Loosely tie it into a pretzel and leave it in the sun or an airy place to dry. This may take a day or two. Unwrap the skirt and shake it out before wearing it out the door.

tips

Clothes with unraveled edges (sometimes called "distressed" or "deconstructed") are featured in many fashion collections.

Shorten an old khaki skirt or create some well-placed holes in jeans, leaving all the edges raw and unfinished. Wash, dry and let nature take its course.

tops

ruched
tube top

curtain lace
tunic

diagonal
halter

baby doll
tunic

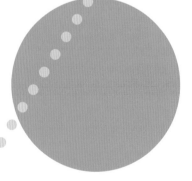

ribbed
tube top

jersey tube
with
drawstrings

t-shaped
jacket

After awhile, tees and camis lose their spark. Heat things up with tubes, tunics and other new tops, sure to set off some fashion fireworks.

ribbed tube top
how-to's on pg. 92

You'll just want to pucker up with this little ruched (gathered) top that adapts to all body types. If you steer away from strapless tops because you prefer to wear a bra, look again. Instructions for this project include removable bra straps that are covered with fabric to match the top.

ruched tube top

ruched tube top

project calculations

Start by grabbing your tape measure and taking your measurements. Flip back to page 16 for details. Fill in the measurements and equations on the blanks provided for ease in figuring out the size of the cut fabric pieces. Follow the labels at each blank to help identify your calculations.

Bust measurement + 50% =A._____

Waist measurement + 3" (7.6cm) = B._____

Measurement B x 11 = C._____

Waist measurement + ½" (1.3cm) =D._____

In order to use the calculator to figure out a number based on a percentage, start by punching in the original number to start, in this case your bust measurement. Push the addition symbol (+). Click on the percentage number, in this case 50. Then, push the percent symbol (%). If you get an uneven number—and in most cases you will—round it up to the nearest whole number. Write this number in the blank for Measurement A.

shopping list

Before you can buy fabric, you need to compare your bust measurement with the width of whatever fabric you've fallen in love with. In many cases, fabric is 45" wide, which is too narrow to cut Measurement A in one piece for most people.

- Fabric, amount to buy determined in the yardage chart.

- ⅛" (3mm) wide elastic, enough to equal Measurement C.

- ½" (13cm) wide elastic, enough to equal Measurement D.

- Thread to match the fabric.

- Removable bra straps (optional).

ruched tube top

If your fabric is not as wide as Measurement A, you'll have to buy enough fabric to stitch an extra piece to the width (see diagram 1). Other fabric comes 54" or 60" (138 or 150cm) wide, which means you don't have to buy as many yards and you don't have to piece extra fabric to the width. Border prints have a lovely printed design along one or both selvages. In this case, you cut ✂ the top sideways (across the grain) and buy a piece of fabric the same length as Measurement A (see diagram 2).

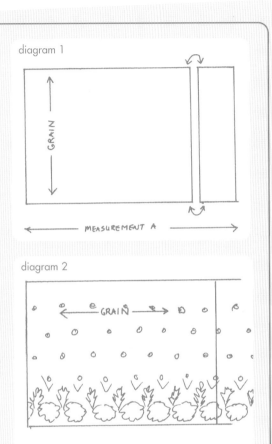

diagram 1

GRAIN

MEASUREMENT A

diagram 2

GRAIN

MEAS. A

bust measurement	fabric width	amount to buy
30" (76.2cm) or less	45" (115cm) or wider	1⅛ yards (1.02m)
30½" (77.5cm) or more	45" (115cm)	2 yards (1.82m)
30½"–36" (77.5–91.4cm)	54" (140cm)	1⅛ yards (1.02m)
36½" (92.7cm) or more	54" (140cm)	2 yards (1.82m)
30½"–40" (77.5–101.6cm)	60" (150cm)	1⅛ yards (1.02m)
30½"–40" (77.5–101.6cm)	border print (cut sideways)	enough to equal Measurement A

cutting

Cut 1 or 2 lengths of fabric each 32" (81.3cm) long.

If your fabric is wide enough for Measurement A and you have only 1 length of fabric, skip the next paragraph.

If you needed enough fabric to cut 2 lengths each 32" (81.3cm) long, pin both pieces with right sides together along the selvages (see diagram 1). Make sure that the print on the fabric (flowers or words, for example) is going in the same

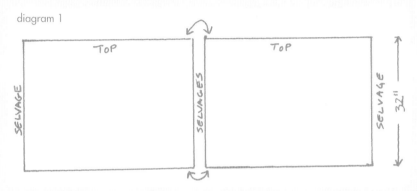

diagram 1

direction on both pieces. Stitch the edges together as pinned, with the seam allowances wide enough to avoid any of the selvages showing in the seam. Trim the selvages away, and leave only a ¼" (6mm) seam allowance. Press the seam allowances to one side.

For all sizes, trim off the selvage at one outside edge. From this edge, measure and mark a panel that's as wide as Measurement A for the final tube top piece. Trim off the excess fabric beyond this point (see diagram 2).

diagram 2

FINAL TUBE TOP PIECE

MEASUREMENT A

If you want bra strap covers, cut 2 strips of fabric from scrap pieces, each 32" long and 2 ½" wide (81.3 x 6.4cm).

ruched tube top

sewing

Use ½" (13mm) seam allowances
unless mentioned otherwise.

1 Lay the tube top piece flat on a table with the wrong side up. Place the 32" (81.3cm) edge vertical to you. With your dressmaker pencil, mark the following places along the short (32" or 81.3cm) sides: 3" (7.6cm) down from the top corners on each side; 17" (43.2cm) up from the bottom corners on each side (see diagram). If you started with 1⅛ yards (1.02m) of fabric, your tube top piece won't have the seam that's shown in the diagram.

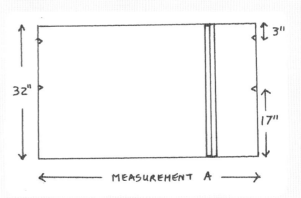

32"

3"

17"

MEASUREMENT A

2 Fold the tube top piece in half, with the sides and marks matching 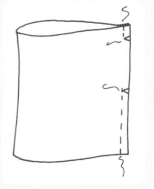 and right sides together . Pin and stitch together these matched edges, leaving an opening between the 2 sets of marks. Make sure to backtack at the beginning and end of each stitching line (see diagram). Press the seam allowances open , including the seam allowances along each edge of the opening.

With wrong sides out, bring the two open (unseamed) edges around to meet. Don't tuck one end of the tube inside the other. Pin the raw edges with the right sides together  and the seam ends matching. In order to pin both edges together entirely around, you'll have to refold the tube, rotating it to bring all the surfaces to the outside (see diagram 1). Stitch the edges together as pinned. Reach inside the opening in the first seam and turn the right sides out . Arrange the tube so that the completed seam is along the bottom edge and the opening in the first seam is on the outside (see diagram 2). This is a little tricky, but you're up to the challenge.

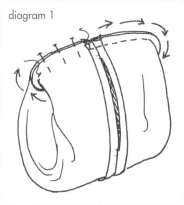

diagram 1

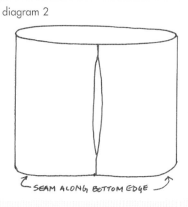

diagram 2

SEAM ALONG BOTTOM EDGE

Along the opening, pin the tube layers together so that the open edges with the folded seam allowances butt closed (no jokes, please). With a large hand stitch, baste through both the outer and inner layers along each side to hold the open edges in place (see diagram).

In this step, you mark the casing channels. In order to control the edges of the opening, you will be placing the fabric under the sewing machine needle with the open side up. This side will eventually be the inside of the tube top, so you can mark stitch lines directly on this side of the fabric with your ruler and dressmaker pencil.

ruched tube top

Mark a stitch line 2 ½" (6.4cm) up from and parallel to the folded bottom edge completely around the tube. Mark another stitch line 1" (2.5cm) above the first stitch line in the same manner around the tube. Continue marking stitch lines at 1" (2.5cm) intervals until you've reached the top. Once you're finished, you should have stitch lines marked for one closed ruffle each at the top and bottom edges with 12 open casings in between (see diagram). To prepare for sewing, place pins around the tube to hold the inside and outside layers together.

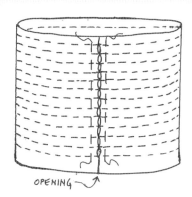

OPENING

If you have a sewing machine with a free arm, keep the inside of the tube turned out and slide the front of the tube onto the free arm under the needle, so that the inside is facing up (see diagram 1). If you don't have a free arm, turn the tube with right sides out so that the opening is on the inside. Slide the back of the tube under the needle and lightly push the front of the tube to the side (see diagram 2).

Sew the bottom stitch line around the tube on the line you marked, beginning and ending at the opening. Continue sewing the stitch lines between the casings, the full length of the tube until you reach the top.

diagram 1

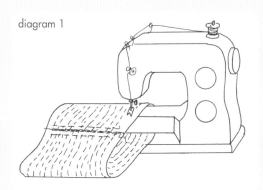

diagram 2

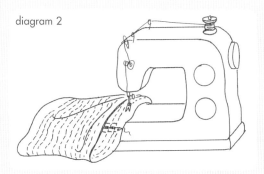

Remove the hand basting that's holding the vertical opening closed. Attach a large safety pin to an end of the ½" (13mm) wide elastic. Insert the pin into the top opening and thread it completely through the casing. Overlap the elastic ends ½" (1.3cm) and pin them together. Once you're sure the elastic isn't twisted, stitch the ends together.

Cut the narrower elastic into 11 pieces, each equal in length to Measurement B. Attach the safety pin to the end of the first piece of the narrower elastic. Insert the elastic in the next casing. Once completely through, loop and knot at about 1½" (3.8cm) from the ends. Continue inserting an elastic length in each casing in this same way. Once all of the elastic pieces are inserted and the ruching is complete, try on the top to see if the elastics are too loose or too tight. Make any adjustments you need. Check to make sure every knot is tied very tightly, then cut off any elastic tails that you don't need.

This step is optional. Hem the short ends of the strap covers by just turning under the raw edges and topstitching them. Fold the strips in half lengthwise, with the right side together , and stitch the long edges using a ¼" (6mm) seam allowance . Attach your trusted safety pin to one end of the cover and turn the tube right side out . Again with the pin, insert a bra strap into each cover. At each end, stitch through all the layers, across the strap, making sure that the hooks extend beyond the cover. Stretch the strap a few times to evenly spread the gathers along the cover. Repeat this step for the other strap. In order to wear the straps, hook them onto your bra. Slide the ruched tube on and pull the top ruffle up so that it covers the bra in the front and the back. The straps aren't attached to the tube, but they look like they are.

If you have a reputation for thinking outside the box, you'll love this tunic because it's fashioned from European-styled curtain lace. This girly top easily dresses up any plain cami or tank. When the tunic is almost complete, string a ribbon through the holes at the top, which were originally provided for a curtain rod. Use extra ribbon for straps and a bow.

curtain lace tunic

curtain lace tunic

Start by grabbing your tape measure and taking your measurements. Flip back to page 16 for details. Fill in the measurements and equations on the blanks provided for ease in figuring out the size of the cut fabric pieces. Follow the labels at each blank to help identify your calculations.

Over bust measurement + 3" (7.6cm) = A._____

Measurement A x 2 = B._____

Measurement A ÷ 2 = C._____

Measurement A ÷ 4 = D._____

shopping list

You may need a certain amount of fabric to go around your body, but plan to buy extra. Café curtain panels often have a fancy pattern woven into the surface, plus decorative scallops along the bottom edge. With extra fabric, you can cut ✂ the tunic so that a pretty pattern in the fabric is centered in the front and the back seam line ends with a complete scallop (see diagram).

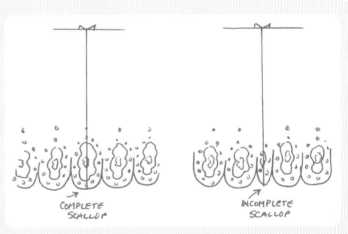

COMPLETE SCALLOP

INCOMPLETE SCALLOP

- Café-length, non-ravel curtain fabric with scallops along a selvage edge, measured and cut as described according to the calculations.

- 3 yards (2.73m) of ⅜" (1cm) wide ribbon.

- 2 sets of flat skirt hooks and bars.

- Thread to match the fabric.

curtain lace tunic

At the fabric store, have the salesperson place the fabric on the cutting table. Measure an amount approximately as long as Measurement A. At this point, fold the fabric back on itself. Pull the top layer a bit more, so that it's slightly longer and the fold is exactly in the center of a scallop. The shaped edges on the top and bottom layers should match. On the top layer, measure from the fold toward the cut edge so that you have enough fabric for Measurement A. Place your finger at this point on the fabric. Now, sliding your finger toward the fabric that's still wrapped on the bolt, stop where the nearest scallop is complete. This point is where the salesperson needs to cut ✂ through the bottom layer of the fabric (see diagram).

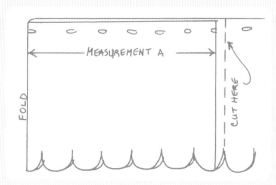

cutting

Along the top (straight) edge of the curtain fabric, cut ✂ a band that's wide enough that the curtain-rod holes are centered along the width (see diagram 1). This top band will be approximately 2" (5cm) wide. Fold the band in half, across the width, and shift it so that the holes match in both layers. Make sure there isn't a hole at the center fold. From the fold, measure enough length to equal Measurement C and cut ✂.

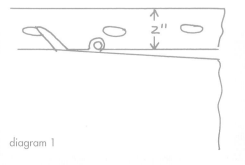

diagram 1

Fold the remaining piece of curtain fabric in half between, or at the center of, a scallop. From the fold, measure a length equal to Measurement A (like you did in the fabric store). To complete the scallop, at the cut fabric edge on the top layer, find the closest point either between two scallops or in the exact middle of a scallop. This is where you'll make a stitching line in a later step. From this stitching line, add a ½" (13mm) seam allowance and cut along this line (see diagrams 2 and 3).

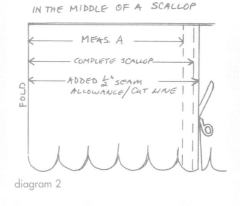

diagram 2

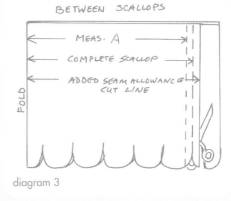

diagram 3

With the fabric still folded, at the top (straight) edge, measure in from the fold a length equal to Measurement D. Mark this point with the dressmaker pencil. We'll call this mark E. At the opposite corner, meas-ure down 2" (5cm) along the cut sides and place a mark. Call it mark G. Measure in from mark G a length equal to Measurement D and mark a point. Call it mark F. Draw a line on the fabric that connects marks E, F, and G. Cut 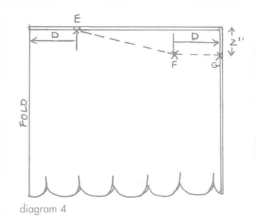 along this line, through both fabric layers (see diagram 4).

Cut 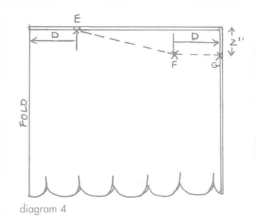 a length of ribbon equal to Measurement A for the band.

diagram 4

curtain lace tunic

sewing

1 Place the band flat on a table with the wrong side up. On the right end, fold ½" (1.3cm) and another ½" (1.3cm) under and pin. On the left end, fold ½" (1.3cm) and another 1" (2.5cm) under and pin. Topstitch along the first folds to finish the hems. Fold the band into 4 parts and mark the folds at the lower edge with pins or the dress-maker pencil. Unfold the band (see diagram).

$$\frac{1}{2}'' + 1''$$

$$1'' \frac{1}{2} + \frac{1}{2}''$$

2 With right sides together 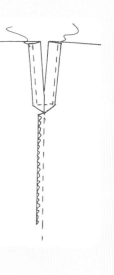, fold the tunic panel in half, matching the side edges. Starting 4" (10.2cm) down from the top edge with a backtack, stitch together the cut ends using a ½" (13mm) seam allowance. The scallop pattern should continue over the seam to make a complete design when the seam is finished and the fabric is opened. From the top corner, measure down 5" (12.7cm) and clip through the seam allowances to within a thread or two of the stitch line. Below the clip, trim the seam allowance to ¼" (6mm) wide. Finish the seam allowances together with zigzag or serge stitching. Above the clip, press the seam allowances back along the opening all the way to the top, and topstitch (see diagram).

Fold the tunic panel into 4 equal parts and mark the folds at the upper edge with pins or the dressmaker pencil. Unfold the panel. Sew a wide basting stitch ¼" (6mm) down from the top edge. Sew another wide basting stitch ½" (1.3cm) down from the top edge. Don't backtack the beginning and end of the basting stitches, but do leave long threads.

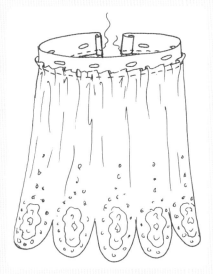

Overlap the top of the tunic on the bottom of the band. Pin the wrong side of the tunic to the right side of the band, matching each quarter mark ◈ , and match the back edges. Gently pull the bobbin threads of the basting stitches to gather up the fullness in the tunic so that it matches the length of the band. Spread the gathers evenly between each pin. Finish pinning the tunic between the basting stitches to the band along the area below the holes. Topstitch the layers together between the basting stitches. Pull the top and bottom basting threads completely out (see diagram).

Thread the cut ribbon from front to back through the first holes on each side of the center front. Continue threading the ribbon ends in and out of the holes until they meet smoothly at the center back. Fold under the ends and tack them to the band. Tack the ribbon in places along the band by hand.

Stitch the 2 skirt hooks to the underside of the band end on the side that has the widest hem. Stitch the bars in corresponding positions on the outside of the opposite end of the band, so that the band ends overlap by ½" (1.3cm).

Try on the tunic. Measure over the shoulder between the ribbon in the front and the back of the band and add 2" (5cm). Use this measurement to cut ◔ 2 straps. Pin the straps to the underside of the band, on the front and back, in an equal distance from the center. Get a friend to help fit the ribbons while you're wearing the tunic. Hand stitch the straps to the ribbon in the band. Tie leftover ribbon into a bow and hand tack it to the center front of the band. Oh, how pretty.

Take one quiet evening and a yard (meter) of fabric, add your sewing machine, and, voilà. . . a new halter appears. If you thought a new wardrobe was harder to make than it was to buy, think again. Ready-to-wear will never look the same again.

diagonal halter

diagonal halter

project calculations

The exact fit of this halter depends on how high and tight you tie the laces. The halter size is based on whatever size T-shirt you wear: extra small, small, medium, large, or extra large.

shopping list

This project calls for fabric that will look good hanging diagonally. Notice that some prints are definitely made to go in a certain direction. You wouldn't want flowers growing upside down, sideways or diagonally over one shoulder.

- 1 yard (.91m) lightweight woven cotton, 44" (115cm) wide.

- 1 yard (.91m) lightweight solid cotton flannel for lining (optional).

- Thread to match the fabric.

Hold your fabric up by one corner and look to see if it works in that position. Consider a solid or a non-directional print such as a symmetrical plaid, geometric, all-over dot . . . you get the idea.

WRONG

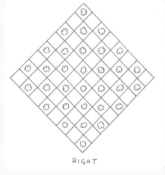

RIGHT

Also, if your halter fabric is thin or a light color, it might be sort of, uh, see-through. (Ouch!) You can still use it—just be modest by adding a layer of lining fabric to give your halter more body. Whatever the weight of your fabric, you might want to include a lining because it'll keep your halter looking better after several rounds in the washing machine.

diagonal halter

cutting

Cut 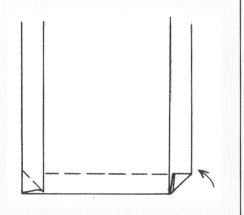 one square each of fabric and lining (if you're adding a lining) based on your T-shirt size:

Size	Halter Square	Lining Square (Optional)
Extra small	22" x 22" (55.9 x 55.9cm)	17½" x 17½" (44.5 x 44.5cm)
Small	24" x 24" (61 x 61cm)	19½" x 19½" (49.5 x 49.5cm)
Medium	26" x 26" (66 x 66cm)	21½" x 21½" (54.6 x 54.6cm)
Large	28" x 28" (71.1 x 71.1cm)	23½" x 23½" (59.7 x 59.7cm)
Extra Large	30" x 30" (76.2 x 76.2cm)	25½" x 25½" (64.8 x 64.8cm)
All sizes	4 strips of fabric, cut from selvage to selvage (across the fabric). Make each strip 1¼" (3.2cm) wide, for the laces.	

Sewing

Place the halter square on your ironing board with the wrong side up. Fold over 2" (5cm) on all four sides and press. Don't forget to miter the corners (see diagram). Check back to page 21 for mitering details. Tuck each raw edge down into the fold on each side to make a double 1" (2.5cm) hem. Press all of the hem edges.

This step is optional: Gently lift the pressed edges and fit the lining square inside the folds along all 4 sides. Pin the hems through all of the layers and topstitch (see diagram).

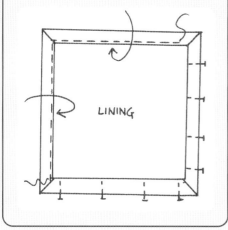

LINING

Decide which corner will be the top. Measure 4" (10.2cm) out from the top corner on each side and mark this spot with the dressmaker pencil (see diagram). Fold down the top point between the marks.

Topstitch ¾" (19mm) from the fold through all the layers to make a casing.

Now you'll need the four fabric strips. Trim the selvages from the ends of each strip. Seam two strips together end-to-end using ¼" (6mm) seam allowances. Press the seam allowances open. You have two fabric strips left. Don't seam them together. Lay one short strip on an ironing board with the wrong side up. Press the long raw edges to the center and then fold the strip again, lengthwise, along the center (see diagram). Stitch along the open edge to make a long thin lace. Repeat the same process for the other short strip and the long, double strip.

diagonal halter

Take one short lace and from it cut ✂ 6 lengths, each 2½" (6.4cm) long. You'll have leftover tie, but that's okay. Fold each little piece in half to make a loop and staystitch the raw ends together. Pin one loop to the wrong side of the halter square, along the upper edge on both side corners (see diagram 1). Pin 2 additional loops above each side loop, 2½" (6.4cm) apart (see diagram 2).

diagram 1

diagram 2

2½"

2½"

Thread the remaining short lace through the casing at the base of the neck. Attach a large safety pin to one short end if you need help pulling the tie through. Thread the longest lace through the top loops at the back and crisscross to the opposite loops. Tie the top lace comfortably around your neck and the back lace around your back waist. Adjust how you wear the halter to fit your body type best. Trim the lace ends if they're uneven. Have fun!

tips

Adapt the diagonal halter instructions by using varied fabric items such as a bandana, silk scarf or lace-edged linen napkin.

Summertime dressing calls for a soft touch. A baby doll tunic blends drapey fabric with cool styling. Custom-fit the bust and midriff by fashioning your own pattern.

baby doll tunic

baby doll tunic

project calculations

Start by grabbing your tape measure and taking your measurements. Flip back to page 16 for details. Fill in measurements and equations on the blanks provided for ease in figuring out the size of cut fabric pieces. Follow the labels at each blank to help identify your calculations.

In order to use the calculator to figure out a number based on a percentage, start by punching in the original number to start, in the first case the bust measurement. Push the addition symbol (+). Click on the percentage number, in this case 33. Then, push the percent symbol (%). If you get an uneven number—and in most cases you will—round it up to the nearest whole number. Write this number in the blank for Measurement A.

For the bust cup portion of the tunic, use your bra cup size.

Bust measurement + 33% = A._____

Measurement A ÷ 2 = B._____

shopping list

- 1¼ yard (1.14m) soft fabric, 44" (115cm) or wider, in a solid or non-directional print.

- Single fold bias binding, ½" (13mm) wide, enough to equal Measurement A.

- Elastic, ⅜" (1cm) wide, long enough to equal your bust measurement.

- Thread to match the fabric.

you'll also need...

- 12"–14" square (30.5–35.6cm) piece of paper.*

*You can tape together printer paper, if necessary, or use an opened brown-paper grocery bag. You need this paper to make a bust cup pattern, so the amount of paper you need could be more or less than suggested.

baby doll tunic

making a pattern

Draw and cut out a paper square with the following dimensions:

Bust cup size A: 12" x 12" (30.5 x 30.5cm)

Bust cup size B: 13" x 13" (33 x 33cm)

Bust cup size C: 14" x 14" (35.6 x 35.6cm)

Draw a line diagonally from the upper left corner to the lower right corner. Cut along the line. You'll only need one triangle, so throw the rest away. Place the remaining triangle on a table with the longest side at the bottom. From each side corner, measure 6" (15.2cm) in along the bottom edge and make a mark (see diagram 1).

diagram 1

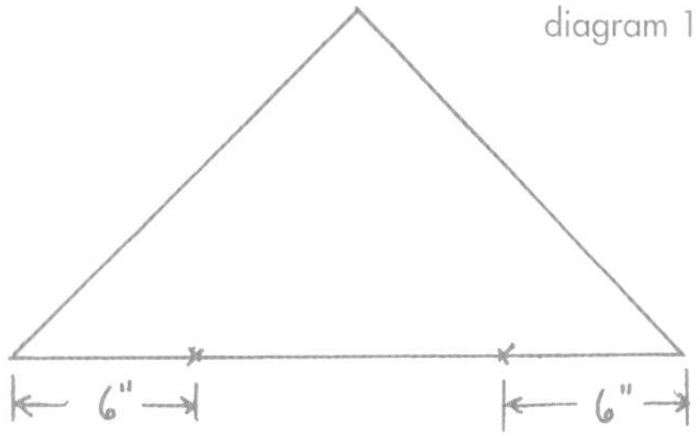

← 6" →   ← 6" →

From each side corner, measure up along the diagonal sides and make a mark at the following measurements:

Bust cup size A: 2" (5cm)

Bust cup size B: 2½" (6.4cm)

Bust cup size C: 3" (7.6cm)

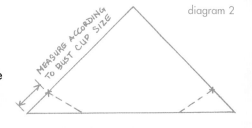

diagram 2

MEASURE ACCORDING TO BUST CUP SIZE

Draw a line between the 2 marks on each side (see diagram 2). Cut the corners off and throw these away.

cutting

Cut 2 rectangles from the fabric, each 17" (43.2cm) long and as wide as Measurement B, for the tunic panels.

Cut 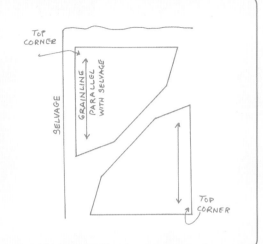 4 bust cups from the fabric, using the triangle pattern that you made. When placing the pattern on the fabric, make sure that one of the sides extending from the top corner is parallel to the selvage of your fabric each time (see diagram). Two of the bust cups will be for the front and 2 for the lining.

Cut 2 ties, each 26" long and 1¼" wide (66 x 3.2cm).

TOP CORNER

SELVAGE

GRAINLINE PARALLEL WITH SELVAGE

TOP CORNER

sewing

Use a ½" (13mm) seam allowance unless mentioned otherwise.

Place each tie strip on an ironing board with the wrong side up. Press the long raw edges to the center and then fold the strip in half lengthwise. Stitch along the matched open edges, to make a narrow tie.

Staystitch one end of each tie to each of the front bust cups, placing the tie at the top corner (see diagram 1). Place a lining cup shape on the bust cup, with right sides together . Stitch a lining to each bust cup along the 2 upper sides. Clip the corner seam allowances and turn each cup right side out through the bottom. Staystitch the bottom sides together, sewing close to the raw edges (see diagram 2).

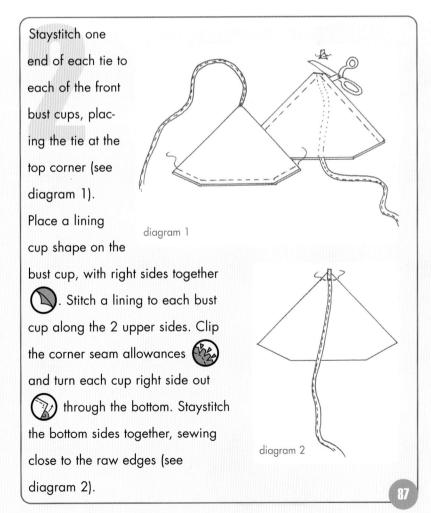

diagram 1

diagram 2

87

baby doll tunic

3 Sew 2 rows of basting stitches along the bottom edge, just between the center marks ⅜" (10cm) and ⅝" (15cm) from the edge. Leave long threads at each end (see diagram).

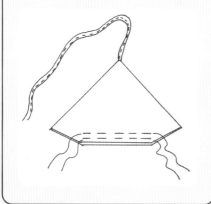

4 Now get out the rectangles for the tunic panels. One is for the front and the other is for the back. On the top edge (equal to Measurement B) of the front tunic panel, find the center point by measuring across the width or folding the rectangle in half. Measure out 1¼" (3.2cm) to each side of the center point and mark each point with your dressmaker pencil. You should have 2½" (6.4cm) in the very center of the front top edge (see diagram).

2½"

FRONT

5 With the raw edges and right sides together ⊘, pin one bust cup to the tunic panel with one corner matching a corner on the top edge of the rectangle and the opposite corner of the same cup matching the mark that's past the center point ⊕. Gently pull the basting stitches at the bottom of the cup, to gather up the bust cup in the center, until it fits along the tunic edge. Staystitch ⅜" (10mm) ⊟ from the raw edge (see diagram).

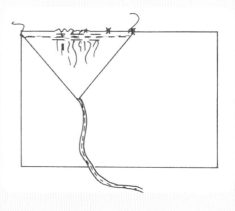

Repeat the same step with the second bust cup on the opposite side of the tunic panel's top edge. In the center, the bust cup corners will overlap (see diagram). Remove all of the basting stitches.

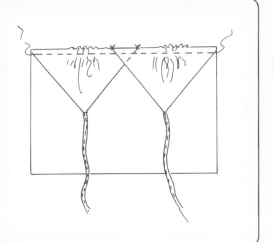

With the right sides together , pin the tunic panel back to the front along the side seams. Stitch from the top corners only 8" (20.3cm) down on each side and backtack to end each seam (see diagram 1). Finish the seam allowance edges separately the full length of the sides with a zigzag or serging stitch. Press the seam allowances open,

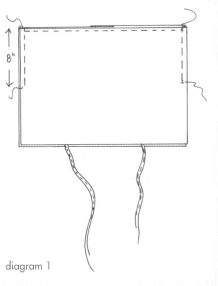

diagram 1

extending the crease down along the unseamed edges, for the slit at each side. Topstitch the seam allowances on each side, ¼" (6mm) from the edges, and across the top of each slit (see diagram 2).

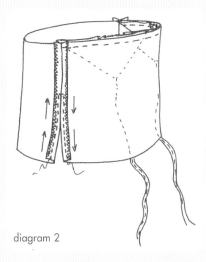

diagram 2

baby doll tunic

Open the fold of the bias binding along one edge. Place the bias binding on the right side of the tunic (it'll be over the bust cup) so that the open fold is ½" (1.3cm) from the raw edge of the tunic. Starting at one side seam, pin the binding completely around the top edge of the tunic with each binding end folded back so they butt at one tunic side seam. The long seam allowances on the binding and tunic won't be the same width, but that's okay. Just shift the binding down ¼" (6mm) and stitch with ½" (13mm) seam allowances (see diagram 1).

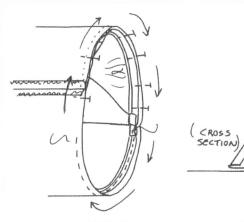

diagram 1

Trim the tunic seam allowance back to the same width as the binding. Press the binding around to the wrong side (inside the tunic) and pin thoroughly. Stitch through all of the layers along the opposite fold of the binding. Press (see diagram 2). Attach a safety pin to an end of the elastic and then thread the elastic through the casing opening where the binding ends meet. Overlap the elastic ends 1" (2.5cm) and stitch.

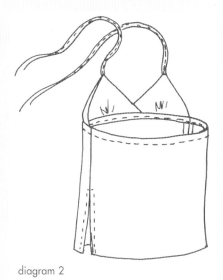

diagram 2

Press 🪧 up the bottom hem ½" (1.3cm) and then 1" (2.5cm). Topstitch along the first fold, through all layers, to finish the hem. Knot the end of each tie. Put on the tunic and tie the ties at the back of the neck into a sweet bow. Your friends will be searching the mall to find where you bought your baby doll tunic. The joke's on them!

Every gal should be able to whip up a cute tube top in one afternoon, so that she can wear it out with her friends that evening. The girls will be so impressed, this DIY diva will be taking orders.

ribbed tube top

(tube top)

A = 43.5
B = 26½
C = 291.5
D = 24"

45" width or wider   (1½ yards)

(Baby Doll tunic)   (shopping list)
                           1½ yd soft fabric
                              44" or wider -
A = 38.57   solid or nondirect
                                  print
B = 19.285   single fold bias bindy ½"
                                          wide
                       _____
                       enough for A
5   elastic 3/8" (1cm) wide
                          29" long 1cm wide
                       thread

Dress ma

⅛" (3mm
8½ yds (8¼/2)2"
½" wide elastic (24")
thread

ribbed tube top

project calculations

Start by grabbing your tape measure and taking your measurements. Flip back to page 16 for details. Fill in measurements and equations on the blanks provided for ease in figuring out the size of cut fabric pieces. Follow the labels at each blank to help identify your calculations.

In order to use the calculator to figure out a number based on a percentage, start by punching in the original number to start, in

Bust measurement + 1½" (3.8cm) = A._____

Measurement A – 40% = B._____

this case Measurement A. Push the subtraction symbol (-). Click on the percentage number, in this case 40. Then, push the percent symbol (%). If you get an uneven number—and in most cases you will—round it up to the nearest whole number. Write this number in the blank for Measurement B.

shopping list

- ⅜ yard (.34m) of stretch fabric that's at least as wide as Measurement A.
- ⅜ yard (.34m) of stretch ribbing that's at least as wide as Measurement B.
- Thread to match the fabric.

cutting

Cut ✂ 1 piece of stretch fabric for the body. The length depends on your height: Cut a length that's 11" (27.9cm) if you're average, 10" (25.4cm) for petite, or 12" to 13" (30.5 to 33cm) for tall. Cut ✂ the body as wide as Measurement A. Make sure the fabric width (Measurement A) is the most stretchy direction. Cut ✂ 2 strips of stretch ribbing along the stretchy edge the same length as Measurement B, each 5" (12.7cm) wide.

ribbed tube top

sewing

All the seam allowances  are ½" (13mm). Flip back to page 18 to see tips on sewing with knit fabrics that stretch.

Fold the stretch fabric in half by bringing the right sides and short edges together. Join the short edges with stretch or zigzag stitching. Trim and finish the seam allowances with zigzag or serging stitches that also stretch, if you want. (see diagram).

Fold one piece of the ribbing in half with the right sides and short edges together. Stitch the same way you did for the stretch fabric. Finger-press the seam allowances open. Refold the ribbing in half lengthwise so that the raw edges are together and the seam allowances are to the inside (see diagram). Thoroughly pin these edges so they don't shift apart. Repeat this step for the other piece of ribbing.

Fold the tube along the seam and, at the opposite fold, mark the top and bottom in the seam allowance with your dressmaker pencil. In the same way, fold each ribbing band along the seam and mark the seam allowance at the opposite fold (see diagram).

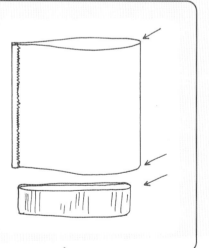

With the raw edges and right sides together 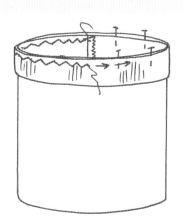, pin a ribbing band to the top edge of the tube. Start by matching the seams, and then match the spots with the pencil marks. The tube will be looser than the ribbing. Gently stretch the ribbing out and pin the edges together the rest of the way around the edges. Starting at the seam, sew the tube and ribbing around the pinned edge with an extra-wide and long zigzag stitch (see diagram). Repeat the same process to stitch the other ribbing band along the bottom edge.

Slip the tube on to see if the ribbing pieces are loose enough to get it on but tight enough to keep the top in place. If you think the ribbing at the top or bottom needs to be tighter, pin it a little tighter to test the fit. Move around to make sure the top works for you. When you know what changes to make, snip the wide zigzag stitches to remove the ribbing. Take in or let out the ribbing along the short seam as much as you need. Join the ribbing to the tube again. When you're sure the top and bottom ribbing pieces are perfect, stitch them to the tube with a final stretch or zigzag stitch, right on top of the wide stitching. Trim and finish off the seam allowances. Steam the tube top with an iron if you want.

Depending on your fabric, this fun top can go dressy or casual. Check out all the pretty stretch fabrics before you make a choice or, better yet, make two.

jersey tube with drawstrings

jersey tube with drawstrings

project calculations

Start by grabbing your tape measure and taking your measurements. Flip back to page 16 for details. Fill in the measurements and equations

Bust measurement = _____

Bust measurement ÷ 2 = A._____

Measurement A + 2" (5cm) = B._____

Waist measurement + ½" (1.3cm) = C._____

on the blanks provided for ease in figuring out the size of the cut fabric pieces. Follow the labels at each blank to help identify your calculations.

shopping list

- T-shirt jersey or other light- or medium-weight *stretch* fabric, width and length as determined in the table.

- ½" (13mm) wide elastic, long enough to equal Measurement C.

- Thread to match the fabric.

bust measurement	fabric width	amount to buy
Up to 35" (88.9cm)	any width	⅞ yard (.8m)
35½" (89cm) or more	44" (115cm)	1⅝ yard (1.48m)
35½" (89cm) or more	54" or 60" (138 or 150cm)	⅞ yard (.8m)

jersey tube with drawstrings

cutting

Cut 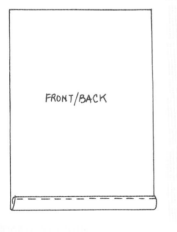 1 front and 1 back panel, each 28" (71.1cm) long and as wide as calculated for Measurement B.

Cut 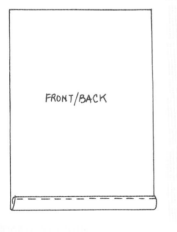 4 drawstrings, each 1¼" wide and 20" long (3.2 x 50.8cm).

sewing

Flip back to page 18 for some tips on sewing with knit fabrics that stretch.

1 On the front and back panels, decide which edges are the top and the bottom. Along the bottom edge of both the front and back panels, press up ½" (1.3cm) and another 1" (2.5cm). Topstitch the hem along the first fold on each panel (see diagram).

FRONT/BACK

2 With right sides together, stitch the front and back panels along the side seams using 1" (25mm) seam allowances. Trim the seam allowances back to ½" (1.3cm) wide on both sides, only for the top 10" (25.4cm) at each seam (see diagram). Press all of the seam allowances open.

10"   10"

Finish the seam allowances with a zigzag-ging or stretch serging stitch if the fabric is likely to run or unravel. At each side, top-stitch the widest seam allowances open, placing the stitching ¾" (1.9cm) from the seam line, to make the draw-string casings. Leave the top and bottom of the casings open (see diagram).

Along the top (unseamed) edge, press 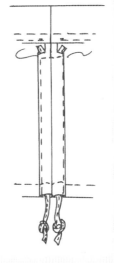 under ½" (1.3cm) and another 3¾" (9.5cm) to the inside. Topstitch along the first fold, leaving a 1" (2.5cm) opening at one side seam. Topstitch again around the top edge 3" (7.6cm) down from the outermost fold (see diagram).

Fold the drawstrings in half lengthwise and press. Tuck the long raw edges into the center fold and press again. Topstitch the drawstrings close to the outside folds. On one drawstring, attach a safety pin to a short end and use it to thread the drawstring through one of the casings at a side seam. Pull the drawstring end slightly out of the casing and pin to all the layers at the top of the casing. In the same way, thread another drawstring through the casing right beside the first one. Topstitch across the seam line and the top of the casing to attach both drawstrings. Knot the drawstring ends (see diagram). Repeat this step for the other two drawstrings and casings on the opposite side.

jersey tube with drawstrings

Pin a safety pin to the end of the elastic and thread it through the casing around the top edge. Overlap the ends, making sure that the elastic isn't twisted, and stitch the ends together. Fold down the top edge over the elastic and try on the top. Once you're happy with the fit, stitch the opening for the top casing closed. Pull the drawstrings evenly on each side and tie them together. Adjust the folds created by pulling the drawstrings. Wasn't that easy?

tips

Borrow the drawstring technique

to revamp a T-shirt, sweatshirt or stretch pants forgotten in the bottom of your drawer. Pick a seam or two suitable for adding a pair of drawstrings.

Stitch single-fold bias tape along each side of the seam allowance on the wrong side to make a double casing. Thread cotton drawstring, ribbon or rayon twist cord through each casing and tack through all the layers at the top.

Pull the drawstrings to cinch up the edge and tie together to hold the new shape.

Based on the same shape as a kimono, this jacket slips over anything from skirts to jeans. Belt it closed or leave it open. This is the kind of lightweight cover-up that comes in handy all the time.

t-shaped jacket

t-shaped jacket

project calculations

Start by grabbing your tape measure and taking your measurements. Flip back to page 16 for details. Fill in measurement on the blank provided for ease in figuring out what size jacket fits you best.

Bust measurement = _____

shopping list

This jacket has sizes calculated in extra small, small, medium, large, and extra large.

In all cases, the finished length is 21" (53.3cm), as measured from the shoulder to the hem. If you want the jacket longer, make the front and back rectangles longer.

- 44" (115cm) or wider fabric that looks good on both sides, 1½ yards (1.37m).
- Thread to match the fabric.

cutting

In order to fit all the jacket pieces on the fabric, open it out into a single layer. Cut 2 front and 1 back rectangles, each 23½" (59.7cm) long and to the widths noted in the table. Also cut 2 sleeves, both according to the measurements shown in the table.

size	to fit bust measurement	jacket part	width	pieces to cut
Extra small	34"	Front	11½" (29.2cm)	2
		Back	21" (53.3cm)	1
Small	36"	Front	12" (30.5cm)	2
		Back	22" (55.9cm)	1

t-shaped jacket

size	to fit bust measurement	jacket part	width	pieces to cut
Medium	39"	Front	12¾" (32.4cm)	2
		Back	23½" (59.7cm)	1
Large	42"	Front	13½" (34.3cm)	2
		Back	25" (63.5cm)	1
Extra large	45"	Front	14¼" (36.2cm)	2
		Back	26½" (67.3cm)	1
All sizes		Sleeve	25" long x 13½" wide (63.5 x 34.3cm)	2

sewing

Place the back rectangle flat on a table with the right side up and the "width" edge at the top. Pin the front rectangles to the back, with right sides together ⬤ and the top edges—or shoulders—matching. The front rectangles will slightly overlap at the center. Using 1" (25mm) seam allowances ⬤, stitch each of the two shoulder seams as pinned, starting at the outside corners and making the seam only 5" (12.7cm) long (see diagram). Don't forget to backtack ⬤ at both ends of the seam, especially at the inner end.

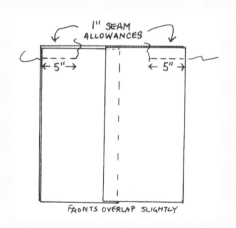

Press the seam allowances open 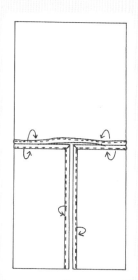, continuing the fold along the neck opening on the front and back pieces. Press the raw edges into the folds, to make a double hem, with a finished width of ½" (1.3cm), along the neck edge and shoulder seam of the front and back pieces. Press another double ½" (1.3cm) deep hem along each vertical edge of the center front opening. Flip back to page 21 to see how to miter the hem allowances in the corners. Topstitch close to the inside fold to finish the neck and front edges (see diagram). Press .

Fold each sleeve in half, matching raw edges of the 13½" (34.3cm) sides. Place a pin on the fold along one edge (see diagram 1) or mark it with the dressmaker pencil.

Open out a sleeve and pin it to a side of the jacket, matching the center mark to the shoulder seam . With right sides together , stitch using a ½" (13mm) seam allowance . Finish the seam allowances so that they're joined together with a zigzag or serging stitch. Press the seam allowances out toward the sleeve. Repeat for the sleeve on the other side (see diagram 2).

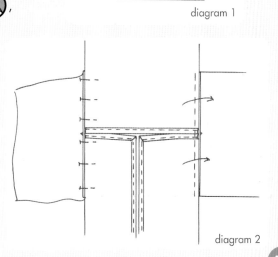

FOLD

diagram 1

diagram 2

t-shaped jacket

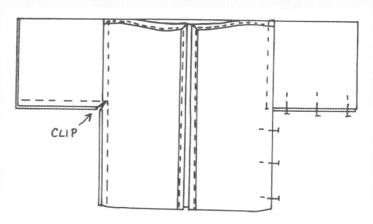

4 Fold the jacket along the shoulder seam, matching right sides together . Pin and stitch the side and sleeve seams together using ½" (13mm) seam allowances. At each underarm, clip the seam allowances to within 1–2 threads of the stitching, without cutting through the seam line (see diagram). Again, finish the seam allowances together the same way you did in the last step.

CLIP

5 Press under ½" (1.3cm) and another 1" (2.5cm) along the bottom edge for a double hem. Topstitch close to the first fold. Repeat the same hemming process for the bottom edges of each sleeve. Press. You can wear this jacket with the front corners together, or flip them back so that they look like lapels. Try shifting the jacket to one side to reveal a little shoulder. It's no hoodie, that's for sure!

tips

Look for fabric that has a different but pretty look on both the right and wrong sides. Flat fell the seams for a reversible jacket.

Extend the jacket length to mid-thigh or so. Wear over a top and leggings, cinched with a belt.

Experiment with appliqué, embroidery or textile painting, embellishing individual pieces before you assemble them into the jacket.

accessories

sheer scarf with appliqués

fleece hat & pompom boa

patchwork tote

ribbon & trim combo belt

slim photo purse

bias sash

two-tone scarf with beaded fringe

denim belt with studs

yarn mesh triangle scarf

Not everyone can spring for a new wardrobe at one time. Pep up your favorite outfits with a new bag, scarf or belt. Let accessories re-energize your look.

two-tone scarf with beaded fringe how-to's on p. 142

Do you love that long-scarf look, but think a clunky muffler isn't exactly your style? Then it's time to try something airy and light. Layer appliqués on both sides of the scarf so that shapes and colors show through.

sheer scarf with appliqués

sheer scarf with appliqués

shopping list

- 1 yard (.91m) fine cotton or other sheer or see-through fabric.
- ⅛ yard (.11m) or remnants of 3 contrasting colors in the same fabric as the main part of the scarf.
- Thread to match the fabric.
- 8 skeins of embroidery floss in any color combinations to match the scarf and appliqués.

you'll also need...

- Old cereal box or other tagboard, for appliqué and tassel patterns. Cut 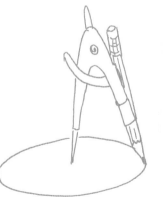 it open so it's out flat.
- Compass for tracing circle appliqués (optional).

making the patterns

Make your tagboard pattern for appliqués by cutting 4 circles of different sizes. You can use a compass to draw circles, 1½", 2", 3" and 4" (3.8, 5, 7.6 and 10.2cm) in diameter (see diagram). If you don't have a compass, just trace around the outside edge of any cup, glass, or small container that's round.

With the same tagboard, make a pattern 3½" (8.9cm) square for the tassels.

cutting

Trim the selvage away from one edge of the main scarf fabric. Cut 2 lengths of fabric along this edge, each 8½" (21.6cm) wide. Trim the ends evenly, making sure that each piece is the same length. Using the remnants of other colored fabrics, cut an assortment of circle appliqués in different sizes and colors.

sheer scarf with appliqués

sewing

Pin the two scarf lengths together along the short ends and stitch using a ½" (13mm) seam allowance 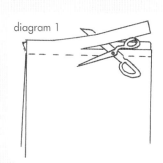. Trim off ¼" (6mm) along one seam allowance only (see diagram 1). Open the scarf lengths and press the remaining seam allowance down, on top of the trimmed seam allowance. Tuck the raw edge of the wider seam allowance under the narrower seam allowance, into the fold, and press both edges nice and flat. Pin the edges as folded. Stitch the fold through all of the layers (see diagram 2). This is called a **flat-felled seam** because it's flat and neat from both the right and wrong sides. Inseams on your jeans are usually flat felled.

diagram 1

diagram 2

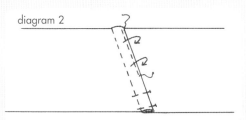

Plan a cool-looking arrangement with 3 or 4 appliqués, starting from each bottom end of the scarf and cascading the appliqués toward the center. Pin the circles thoroughly. Flip the scarf over and pin a contrasting arrangement of the same number of circles on the other side of each scarf end. Using the same thread as on the center scarf seam, carefully stitch a little in from the cut edges around every circle (see diagram). The smaller the circle, the slower and more carefully you'll have to run the sewing machine. Remove or rearrange pins if they get in the way. Go ahead and stitch through layers to create dimension. Now hold up the scarf and see the colors and shapes as the light shines through the fabric. Press the appliqués nice and smooth.

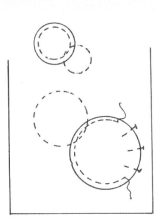

Fold all the outer scarf edges under ¼" (6mm) and again another ¼" (6mm). Press 🔲. Complete the narrow hem by stitching along the inside fold around all four edges. Miter the hem allowance and pivot at each corner. (Flip back to page 21 to see how.) Don't worry which side and which appliqué arrangement you turn the hem toward. It's all random and adds to the design. Press 🔲 all the edges flat.

Thread tassels are easy to make. Cut ✂ 2 lengths of floss, each 8" (20.3cm) long. These are for wrapping the top of the tassel. You can use one or two colors. Keep them handy. Starting at the bottom, wrap a new piece of floss around the tassel pattern 8 complete times. If you're combining different colors of floss, make sure each color begins and ends at the bottom of the tassel pattern. Combine colors in whatever blend you want for a total of 8 complete wraps. Slide one 8" (20.3cm) piece through the coil of the wrapped threads along the pattern. Tie and knot the wrap ends together securely at the top, letting the tails hang down with the other threads, which are still wrapped (see diagram 1). To remove the pattern, cut ✂ the wrapped threads at the end of the pattern that's opposite to the tied end. Wrap the remaining 8" (20.3cm) piece

diagram 1

around the tassel threads about ½" (1.3cm) down from the top (see diagram 2). Knot the ends of the wrapped floss securely and let the ends hang into the tassel. Trim ✂ all of the ends even with the tassel threads. Make 10 tassels altogether.

diagram 2

Hand stitch 5 tassels evenly spaced along each short end of the scarf (see diagram). Wear your scarf around your head, neck, waist, or wherever you like.

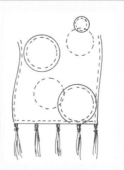

When the temperature drops and there's a chill in the air, you'll be looking for something new to warm up your wardrobe. Pair a cozy hat and pompom boa in easy-to-sew polar-type fleece.

fleece hat & pompom boa

fleece hat & pompom boa

project calculations

Start by grabbing your tape measure and taking your measurements. Flip back to page 16 for details. Fill in the equation on the blank provided for ease in figuring out the size of the cut fabric pieces. Follow the label to help identify your calculation.

Head measurement + 1" (2.5cm) = A._____

shopping list for hat and boa

- ½ yard (.46m) of 60" (150cm) wide polar-type fleece for hat crown and boa.

- ⅜ yard (.5m) of 60" (150cm) wide polar-type fleece for hat brim and boa.

- Thread to match one or both fabrics.

you'll also need...

- Piece of ordinary printing paper.

making patterns

From the paper, cut ✂ a rectangle 6" x 3" (15 x 7.5cm), to make the pompom pattern.

cutting for the hat

Cut ✂ 1 piece of crown fleece 16" (40.5cm) long and as wide as Measurement A.

Cut ✂ 1 piece of brim fleece, 6" (15cm) long and as wide as Measurement A.

Cut ✂ 1 strip of crown fleece, ⅜" wide and 18" long (1 x 45.5cm). Cut the strip in the direction with the least amount of stretch.

fleece hat & pompom boa

cutting for the boa

Cut ✂ 20 pompom rectangles in each color (40 rectangles altogether). Make sure to place the long side of the pattern parallel to the edge of the fleece that has the most stretch.

sewing the hat

For tips on sewing and pressing polar-type fleece, flip back to page 19.

Fold the large crown rectangle in half with the short edges and right sides together. Stitch these edges with a ½" (13mm) seam allowance. Fold the brim rectangle in half with the short edges and right sides together. Stitch in the same manner as the crown. Finger-press the seam allowances open.

With the right sides together, pin one edge of the crown to one edge of the brim and stitch using a ¼" (6mm) seam allowance (see diagram 1). Open the layers and fold the brim piece totally to the wrong side of the crown piece. Now roll the pieces along the seam line so that the crown piece wraps around the seam allowances at the seam. The wrong sides should be together, and the seam line is about ⅜" (1cm) below the folded edge on the inside (see diagram 2). Stitch in the seam around the entire circle to make an edging or faux cord around the brim (see diagram 3).

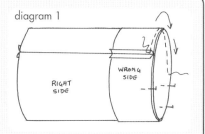

diagram 1

RIGHT SIDE

WRONG SIDE

diagram 2

WRONG SIDE

RIGHT SIDE

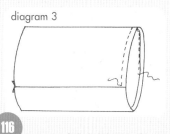

diagram 3

On the opposite edge of the brim, stitch around through both the crown and brim layers ¼" (6mm) from the cut edge (see diagram). You might need to pin this edge first to keep it from shifting around.

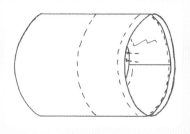

Turn the crown right side out . Cut the opposite raw edge of the crown completely into fringes, each one 3" (7.5cm) long and approximately ⅜" (1cm) wide. Cinch the base of the fringes at the top of the crown by tying and knotting it securely with the remaining fleece strip (see diagram). Trim the strip ends to equal the length of the fringes. Fold up the brim approximately 3" (7.5cm), or as much as you like.

sewing the boa

Pin the pompom rectangles in sets of 2 of the same color, with the wrong sides together. You should have 10 sets of each color for a total of 20 pompom sets. Start with one set and stitch through both layers down the center of the rectangle lengthwise. Don't forget to backtack at the beginning and end of the stitching (see diagram). Repeat for each set in both colors.

Place a stitched rectangle flat on a table. With your fabric scissors, cut fringes from the long edge to the center stitching line (see diagram). Don't cut through the stitching. Continue cutting , making each fringe ⅜" (1cm) wide. Take a good look at your ruler to see how wide this is. You might mark each line if you want, but try to eyeball the width if you can. Repeat the cutting along both sides of each pompom set.

fleece hat & pompom boa

3 Roll up a rectangle along the stitching line (see diagram). Using a needle and matching double thread, hand sew the roll together securely through the middle stitching line about 5 or 6 times. Take a final loose stitch and bring the needle through the last thread loop, pulling the needle tightly to make a knot. Make a second knot in the same manner and trim the thread. Repeat for each pompom.

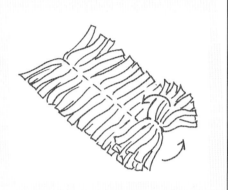

4 Take one pompom and lap a single fringe over one fringe on a contrasting pompom. Machine stitch through the connecting fringes and backtack securely. Repeat with each pompom in alternating colors until all the pompoms are connected together (see diagram).

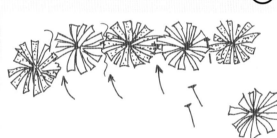

tips crazy for pompoms

Once you've mastered the fine art of pompom-making, consider other ways to use pompoms to decorate your stuff.

- **hair accessory** Take one pompom and tie 2 fringes around a thread-covered rubber band to pop up your usual ponytail.

- **curtain tie backs** Split the boa in half to make 2 shorter lengths. Tie back your bedroom curtains with the boa tie backs in colors to match the rest of your private sanctuary.

- **lapel rosette** Stitch a safety pin to the back of one pompom. Leave the pompom fluffy or softly flatten in the center and glue a cluster of beads to make a rosette brooch.

- **pillow trim** Tack a pompom to each corner of a plain square throw pillow for a variation on the usual tassel or ruffle.

It's time to dig out your favorite scraps of brocade, velvet, and ribbon. An irresistible mix of texture and color does double-duty as a purse or tote. This is just the project you've been waiting for.

patchwork tote

patchwork tote

cutting

Cut 4 squares from the medium-weight fabric, each 13" x 13" (33 x 33cm). 2 squares will be the base for mounting the patchwork and the other 2 squares are for the lining.

Cut assorted decorative fabrics into squares and rectangles, each 4½" (11.4cm) long, in a variety of widths from 2½"–5" (6.4–12.7cm) wide. You'll need enough squares to cover both of the 13" square base fabric pieces.

Cut 4 pieces of ribbon, each 13" (33cm) long.

Cut 2 pieces of fleece, each 13" (33cm) square.

Cut 2 strips of medium-weight fabric, each 4" x 27" (10.2 x 68.6cm), for the straps.

Cut 2 pieces of interfacing, each 4" x 27" (10.2 x 68.6cm), for the straps.

sewing

Use a ½" (13mm) seam allowance unless other-wise mentioned.

Piece together an assortment of patches in a random arrangement along the 4½" (11.4cm) edges until you have a strip approximately 3 yards (2.73m) long (see diagram).

4½"

patchwork tote

2 Place one base square on top of a fleece square with the right side up. Baste the layers together around the outside edges. You won't see the base fabric after the tote is finished. The layers provide a firm surface for mounting the patches. Place the square flat on a table, again with the fabric side up. Lay the patched strip along the bottom of the square, cutting 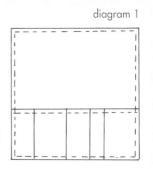 the strip to fit. Staystitch the patched strip around all four of the edges to the base (see diagram 1). Repeat the same step to apply a patched strip along the top edge of the square (see diagram 2).

diagram 1

diagram 2

3 Cut 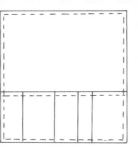 a third patched strip for the center of the square. Pin it in place, slightly overlapping the edges of the strips above and below. Staystitch the center strip along the raw edges (see diagram).

4 Pin a ribbon over each of the two raw edges (see diagram). Stitch the ribbon through all the layers along both long sides. Repeat steps 2, 3 and 4 for the other base square.

With right sides together 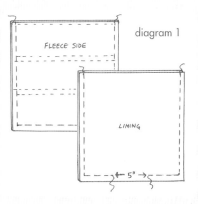, stitch the front and back of the bag along the side and bottom edges. Repeat this same step with the lining pieces, only leave a 5" (12.7cm) opening along the bottom edge for turning the bag later (see diagram 1).

diagram 1

FLEECE SIDE

LINING

←— 5" —→

Starting with the outside of the tote, reposition one corner so that the side seam is folded over the bottom seam.

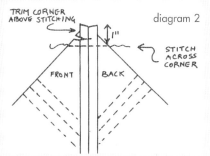

TRIM CORNER
ABOVE STITCHING

diagram 2

1"

STITCH
ACROSS
CORNER

FRONT   BACK

Measure down 1" (2.5cm) from the corner point and draw a line perpendicular to the seam. Stitch across the corner along this line and trim 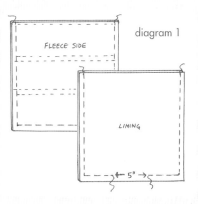 the corner away. Square off the other corner on the bag and the remaining corners on the lining in this same manner (see diagram 2).

patchwork tote

Fuse 🔲 the interfacing to the wrong side of both strap pieces. With right sides together 🔲, join the strap pieces end-to-end to make an extra-long strap. Press the seam allowances open 🔲. Fold the strap in half lengthwise with right sides together 🔲 and pin the long raw edges. Stitch. Attach a safety pin through one layer at an end and use it to turn the strap right side out 🔲 (see diagram). It's a long distance to turn, but you should have plenty of room. Once you're finished turning, press 🔲 the strap neatly with the seam along one edge.

Leave the bag with the wrong sides out. Pin the strap ends to the seams on each side. Make sure the strap isn't twisted. Stitch the straps to the bag where they're pinned (see diagram). Turn the lining right side out 🔲 and fit it down into the bag so that the right sides are together 🔲. Pin the bag and lining together around the top edge (with the strap sandwiched between the layers). Stitch around this edge. Turn the right sides out 🔲 through the opening in the lining. Topstitch the opening closed. Tuck the lining back inside the bag and press the upper edge. You can topstitch all the layers around the opening, too, to hold it in place.

STRAPS

tips

sewing and pressing velvet

Sewing on velvet can be tricky. When you put the right sides together , the little hairs that stand on end, called the **pile**, make it hard to match the stitch lines edge-to-edge. They tend to slide around. You also need to be careful when pressing velvet in order to keep the pile standing up. To make things easier, here are some tips:

- Pin the seam edges together very thoroughly, and only remove pins as you sew along. Although it's good to use pins on any sewing step, don't leave them in velvet overnight because they could leave marks by pressing down in the soft pile. It's nearly impossible to get the pin marks out the next day.

- Reduce the pile by creating your own unique crushed velvet. Experiment with the iron and a piece of scrap fabric. From the wrong side, scrunch up the velvet and press it randomly to add gorgeous texture.

- On the wrong side of the fabric, press the velvet pile down completely to make it look like panné velvet.

- When ironing, use a scrap piece of velvet as a press cloth for velvet projects. Place the sides with the pile together and lightly steam the seams without pressing too hard.

Take a stroll down the ribbon or trim aisle in the fabric store and let your imagination run wild. There are so many possible combinations of trims that look great together. Stack two or three braids, laces or rickracks on top of each other to see how they'll blend. Let your accessories express your originality.

ribbon and trim combo belt

ribbon and trim combo belt

shopping list

- 1¼ yards (1.14m) each of 2 or 3 coordinating braids, ribbons, or trims, in different widths that can be seen when they're stacked together. Make sure the bottom layer is 1¼" or 1½" (3.2 or 3.8cm) wide.

- 1¼ yards (1.14m) grosgrain ribbon, webbing, or belting, the same width as the widest trim, for a base to hold the layers together.

- 1 set of 1¼" (3.2cm) wide D-rings (2 rings in a set).

- Thread to match the fabric.

cutting

Even up the ends of all your trims by cutting them to be all the same length.

sewing

Place the top 2 trims together as they will appear on the belt. If you are using only 2 trims, machine stitch the layers together. If you are using 3 trims, baste the first 2 layers by hand. Pin to the third layer and machine stitch. The trims you chose will determine if you stitch in the center or along both sides. Use your judgment and, if necessary, do a small sample to see how it looks.

ribbon and trim combo belt

2 With right sides together 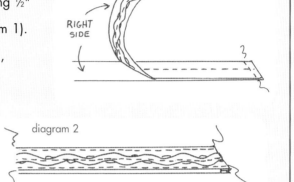, stitch the stacked trims to the base layer, only at one end, using ½" (13mm) seam allowances (see diagram 1). Turn the trim and base right sides out , bringing the wrong sides around together. Make sure the long edges are lined up evenly. Machine stitch the top and base layers together along each side (see diagram 2).

diagram 1

RIGHT SIDE

diagram 2

3 Slip the opposite end with the raw edges through both of the D-rings. At the short end, fold under ½" (1.3cm) and again 1" (2.5cm). Topstitch through the layers to hold the D-rings in place (see diagram). You made this belt so fast, you'll be running back to the store to find more trim combinations to make a drawer-full of belts!

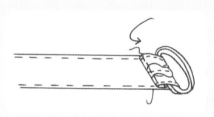

tips   trim try-outs

As you start to see trim combinations take on their own unique look, experiment with different ways to layer and stitch trims together.

- Offset the top layer slightly to one side to see more of the under layer.
- Stitch with contrasting color thread.
- Set your sewing machine to sew with any decorative stitch for layering.
- Zigzag over soutache or rattail cord on top of another layer. This technique is called **couching**.
- Apply lace or a scalloped trim along the edge of a ribbon.
- Thread narrow ribbon or decorative cord through lace.

What a way to show off all the cool pictures you're taking with your digital camera! Just print your photo onto a printable fabric sheet and then appliqué it to the front of a super-skinny bag. Start with a favorite photo of your vacation, sweetheart, BFF or pet. You can make the bag vertical or horizontal to fit whatever photo you choose.

slim photo purse

slim photo purse

shopping list

- ⅜ yard (.34m) fabric, any width, for the outside front and back of the purse.

- ⅜ yard (.34m) fabric, any width, for the gussets.

- ⅜ yard (.34m) fabric, any width, for the lining.

- ¼ yard (.23m) of ⅛" (3mm) thick heavy interfacing stabilizer* with fusing on both sides.

- ¼ yard (.23m) craft- or medium-weight fusible interfacing.

- 1 or 2 sheets of printable fabric sheets.

- Approximately 1 yard (.91m) of ½" (13mm) wide ribbon, rickrack, or trim.

- Paper-backed fusible tape, ⅝" (16mm) wide.

- 1" (2.5cm) of ¾" (2.8cm) wide hook-and-loop tape such as Velcro®.

- 1¼ yard (.14m) of ¼" (6mm) or ⅜" (1cm) wide decorative twisted cord, for the strap.

- Thread to match the fabric.

*At the fabric store, ask for stabilizer usually sold for making fabric bowls or hat brims.

you'll also need...

- 3-4 sheets of ordinary printing paper for making patterns.

- Clear tape (for the horizontal photo only).

- Digital image no larger than 5½" x 6½" (14 x 16.5cm) in a computer file or on a disc.

- Access to a computer and printer.

making the patterns

On a sheet of paper, draw and cut out a rectangle that's 7" x 8½" (17.8 x 21.6cm). This is the base and lining for the front and back. Label this pattern #1.

On another sheet of paper, draw and cut out a rectangle that's 8" x 9½" (20.3 x 24.1cm). This is the gusset. Label this pattern #2.

slim photo purse

picture with a horizontal or landscape format

Tape the last 2 sheets of paper together. Draw and cut out a rectangle 9½" x 10" (24.1 x 25.4cm). Mark a 10" (25.4cm) edge as the top. This is the outside of the front and back. Label this pattern #3.

Take the gusset (#2) and mark one of the 9½" (24.1cm) edges as the top. Measure 2¼" (5.7cm) inside the side and bottom edges and draw a second set of lines. Cut out 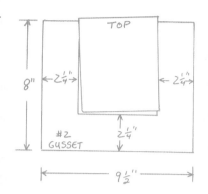 the inside rectangle and throw it away (see diagram).

picture with a vertical or portrait format

On one remaining sheet of paper, draw and cut out 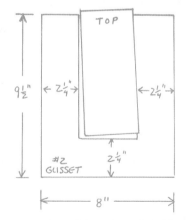 a rectangle 8" x 10¾" (20.3 x 27.3cm). Mark one of the 8½" (21.6cm) edges as the top. This is the outside of the front and back. Label this pattern #3. You won't need the fourth piece of paper.

Take the gusset (#2) and mark the 8" (20.3cm) edge as the top. Measure 2¼" (5.7cm) inside the side and bottom edges and draw a second set of lines. Cut out the inside rectangle and throw it away (see diagram).

cutting

Cut the following parts from the patterns and fabrics listed:

pattern	fabric or other supply	pieces to cut
#1	Lining**	2
#1	Interfacing stabilizer	2
#2	Gusset fabric**	2
#2	Craft-weight interfacing	2
#2	Lining**	2
#3	Outside front and back purse fabric**	2

**Remember to cut fabric pieces so that any print or design in the fabric is horizontal or vertical, depending on the style of purse that you're making.

preparing the photo

Once you've picked the photo that you want to print, make sure you have it in a final size and resolution. Read over the manufacturer's directions for the printable fabric sheets. All brands are different. Make sure you pay attention to the way that you press and set the color on the fabric. Print the photo onto a fabric sheet and permanently set the ink according to the instructions. You only need one printed image. If you bought the second sheet of printable fabric, use it to reprint your image in case of a mistake or save it for another project. Trim the fabric around the outline of the photo and set it aside.

slim photo purse

sewing

Use ½" (13mm) seam allowances unless mentioned otherwise.

Take the outside front and back (cut with pattern #3) and finish the raw side and bottom edges with a zigzag or serge stitch. Leave the top edge alone.

Place a lining piece that was cut from pattern #1 on top of a piece cut from the interfacing stabilizer, matching the outside edges. (The right side of the lining should be facing up, with the edges matching exactly.) Place the outside purse front on top of the lining and stiffener, centered along the top edge with the right side down and the raw edges matching. Stitch all the layers together along the top edge (see diagram). Repeat the same steps for the purse back.

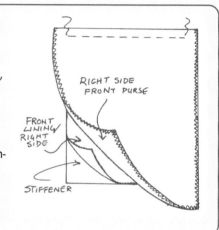

RIGHT SIDE
FRONT PURSE

FRONT
LINING
RIGHT
SIDE

STIFFENER

On the purse front, open the outside layer out flat, and away from the other layers. Stitch one side, of the Velcro® below the stitch line, in the center, through both the interfacing stabilizer and the lining (see diagram). Repeat this step with the purse back and the corresponding piece of Velcro®.

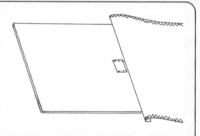

Wrap the front outside layer around the edge of the stabilizer to the opposite side of the purse front. The seam line is set in on the lining side, and the stiff stabilizer itself remains flat. Fuse 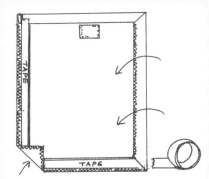 the lining and the outer front to opposite sides of the stabilizer according to the manufacturer's directions.

Place the lining side up. Fuse the fusible tape along the edges of the outer front that extend beyond the edges of the stabilizer layer, on the wrong side only. Read over the directions from the manufacturer to find out how to do this. Remove the paper from the fusing. Fold the corner fabric over to the lining side at an angle, and fold the side and bottom edges over to neatly finish the sides with mitered corners (see diagram). Repeat this step for the purse back.

Flip over the front so that you aren't looking at the piece of Velcro®. Place the photo on the outside of the front. How does it fit? Crop or trim  the sides of the photo to fit on the purse front however you like. Stitch the photo to the front through all the layers. Cover the photo stitching by sewing the trim around the outside edge of the photo. Fold under beginning and end of the trim to butt the joined ends together neatly along the lower edge of the photo (see diagram).

slim photo purse

Fuse 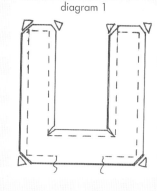 an interfacing piece to the wrong side of a piece of gusset. With right sides together , stitch the gusset to the matching lining completely around the outside edges, leaving a 4" (10.2cm) opening along the bottom. At the outer corners, trim the seam allowances (see diagram 1). At the inside corners, clip the seam allowances carefully to within a thread or two of the stitching. Turn the right sides out through the opening.

diagram 1

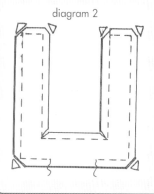

diagram 2

Gently push out the outer corners by pushing from the inside with something that isn't very sharp, like a pencil with a broken point or a pen with a retracted point (see diagram 2). Press the gusset nice and flat.

Place one gusset on a table with the right side up. Tie knots in each end of the strap cord. Pin the cord ends ½" (1.3cm) below the top of the gusset, with the knots beyond the inner edge. Staystitch the cording ends to the gusset, close to the edge (see diagram 1). Place the other gusset piece on top with the right sides together

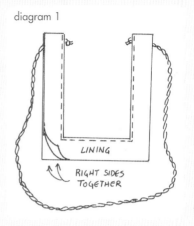

diagram 1

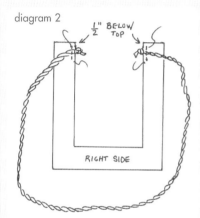

diagram 2

. Stitch through all the layers close to the inner edge. Make sure to backtack at each top edge (see diagram 2).

Place the purse back flat on a table with the lining side up. Place the gusset on top and match the edges. Beginning and ending with a backtack , topstitch the back gusset edge to the purse back ¼" (6mm) from the outside edges (see diagram). Place the purse front with the photo flat on a table and the lining side up. Flip the gusset over to match the opposite edges with the front and topstitch around the edges in the same manner as the back. Lightly press the purse from the back if necessary. The first time you use this purse, everyone will notice!

If you like the soft curve of a necktie belt, consider a sash as a feminine alternative. Because it's bias cut, the sash will drape around your waist or hips in the same way—only you get to make it out of any fabric you want.

bias sash

bias sash

shopping list

- ½ yard (.46m) of 44" (115cm) wide medium-weight fabric that will look good when cut diagonally, such as a stripe or geometric print.

- Thread to match the fabric.

you'll also need...

- Piece of ordinary paper for printing to make a template for cutting the ends at a 45° angle.

cutting

Fold the paper diagonally, to match one short edge and one long edge (see diagram 1). Cut along the fold. Use this cut edge as a guide for a 45° angle.

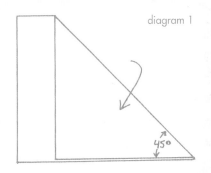

diagram 1

Place the fabric wrong side up on a table. Line up the paper guide in one corner. With a yardstick, draw a line along the side of the guide and extend the line as far as possible to the opposite selvage edge (see diagram 2).

Remove the guide and draw another line, parallel to the first line and 6" (15.2cm) away (see diagram 3). Cut out the sash strip along both lines, from selvage to selvage.

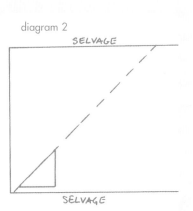

diagram 2

SELVAGE

SELVAGE

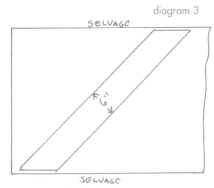

diagram 3

SELVAGE

SELVAGE

bias sash

Use ½" (13mm)

seam allowances

.

Fold the sash strip in half lengthwise, taking care not to stretch the edges. Pin together the 2 edges very generously, to prevent them from shifting apart. Use the paper guide as a pattern for marking the ends at an angle. Trim 🔪 the short ends along the markings. Stitch all of the raw edges together, leaving a 4" (10.2cm) opening in the middle of the sash.

Clip the seam allowances 🔪 at the end points and corners (see diagram). Turn the right sides out 🪡 through the center opening. Use the end of a pen with a retracted point to gently push out the points at each end. Press 🗝 the sash and slipstitch the opening closed. Wear the sash through belt loops with jeans, or cinched around a top or dress. Tie the ends together in a square knot or a one-loop bow. Cute!

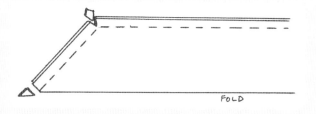

FOLD

tips scoring points with biases

When stitching a tube shape cut on the bias as you do with this sash, or applying bias bindings that you'll find in other projects in this book, be careful that the biased edges don't warp (or twist) as you stitch. This happens when the top side of the biased tube moves under the needle area a thread or two slower than the underside. This is caused by the top layer dragging on the presser foot.

The thicker the fabric, the more likely the top layer could slip back. The sash might look slightly wrinkled if this happens, but no amount of pressing can correct a warped bias. You have to pick out the stitches and go back to the starting line.

In addition to pinning generously, which was recommended in Step 1, here are some other tips:

- Release the pressure on the presser foot (see your sewing machine manual to find out how to do this).
- Use a walking foot or dual feed if you have this with your machine.
- Gently push or ease the top layer of the fabric toward the needle as the fabric feeds through to counteract the direction of the presser foot.
- When all else fails, baste the edges together before stitching.

Understanding biases and stitching a nice biased tube is a big score in the game of sewing. Congratulations! You are ready to pass to the next level.

This simple but elegant scarf can be whipped up in an evening. Everyone will ask you where you bought it. Just smile to yourself. They'll keep wondering.

two-tone scarf with beaded fringe

two-tone scarf with beaded fringe

shopping list

- 1 yard (.91m) polyester crepe or other fabric that handles and feels like a scarf and drapes nicely.

- 1 yard (.91m) contrasting-color fabric with a similar drape to the first fabric.

- ½ yard (.46m) beaded fringe, spangles, or other cool trim for the edges.

- Thread to match the color of both fabrics.

you'll also need...

- A little piece of tape to stick on the ends of the fringe ribbon so that the threads and beads don't come loose.

cutting

On both pieces of the scarf fabric, straighten the cut edges (perpendicular to the selvage) by trimming ✂ any unevenness as little as possible, making sure both pieces of fabric are the same length. Sometimes with scarf-weight fabric, individual project pieces are easier to rip than to cut ✂. Check back to page 30 for tips on ripping.

On one piece of fabric, cut ✂ or rip a selvage the full length of one side. Measuring in from the edge that used to have the selvage, cut ✂ or rip 2 scarf strips, each 8" (20.3cm) wide by the full length of the fabric piece.

Cut ✂ or rip 2 equal scarf strips from the second piece of fabric in the same manner.

two-tone scarf with beaded fringe

Take one fabric strip from each color. With right sides together 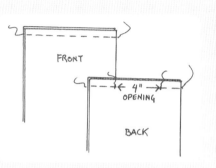, pin the short ends and stitch. This will be the front of the scarf. Repeat to join the remaining lengths for the back of the scarf, leaving a 4" (10.2cm) opening in the center of the seam (see diagram). This opening will be used later to turn the scarf right sides out. Press the seam allowances open on both the scarf front and the scarf back, including along the opening on the back.

beaded fringe 4-1-1 Take a good look at the beaded fringe. It's made with intricate combinations of different beads, hand stitched in a pattern that's attached to ribbon or twill tape. The ribbon holds the fringe together and provides an edge to stitch through. You'll barely see the ribbon when you're finished with this project. You need to stitch very close to the top bead and use a zipper foot on your sewing machine. Don't try to stitch directly through the fringe or something will break: the bead, the sewing machine needle, or both. Also, when you cut the fringe, stick tape on the bead thread to keep it from coming loose, which would cause the beads to fall off. When you backtack at each end, catch the bead thread in the seam before you remove the tape.

Place the scarf front on a table with the right side up. Starting at one end, place the fringe ribbon completely on top of the seam allowance. Pin the fringed edge of the ribbon slightly inside the stitch line on the scarf end, especially if the ribbon is narrower than your ½" (13mm) seam allowance. With a zipper foot, staystitch the ribbon to the scarf end, back-tacking over the bead thread (see diagram).

TAPE ENDS TO CATCH BEAD THREADS

Place the back of the scarf over the front, with the opposite colors and right sides together , and pin around the edges. While your zipper foot is still in your machine, stitch each end along the seam line, as close to the top beads as possible.

With your normal sewing machine foot, stitch along each long edge. Before you are tempted to turn the scarf right sides out through the opening, press the seam allowances perfectly flat around all the edges. This helps the edges look neat and crisp once the right sides are turned out. Clip the corner seam allowances .

Turn the scarf right sides out through the opening in the seam in the center of the back. Very gently pull the fringes out at each end and press the scarf ends. Just to be safe, steer clear of them when pressing. Roll the long edges of the scarf so that the seam is right on the outside edge and you can't see the underside color peeking out. Press all the edges neatly (see diagram).

Slipstitch the opening closed in the center seam on the back. Press again if you want. Wear your scarf tied or hanging loose and watch the colors flutter as you move.

BACK

Denim with studs never goes out of style. You can choose from a wide selection of colors, weights, and even printed denim at your local fabric store. However, if you are looking for an excuse to cut up your old straight-legged jeans, this belt is a good one. Add a few studs with grommet openings for a fresh look, whether your denim is recycled or not.

denim belt with studs